"This is my Alaska..."

"I am well acquainted with the wilderness trails of this wonderful state. I have climbed the mountains and fished the streams, and I have rejoiced in the privilege of hiking the remote areas and camping beside the still lakes.

"Many mornings I have put off breakfast on the trail just to see the glorious sunrise of a new day. I am eternally thankful for the many evenings I have been able to stand on a high place and watch the awesome splendor of an Alaskan sunset..."

Dan Saunders

ALASKA
Memoir of a Vanishing Frontier

AVON
PUBLISHERS OF BARD, CAMELOT, DISCUS, EQUINOX AND FLARE BOOKS

ACKNOWLEDGMENT

I am deeply grateful to Betty Huey Saunders, an author in her own right, without whose help this book would never have been written.

For her inspiration, guidance, and most generous help, I wish to say thanks with all my heart.

ALASKA: MEMOIR OF A VANISHING FRONTIER is an original publication of Avon Books. This work has never before appeared in book form.

AVON BOOKS
A division of
The Hearst Corporation
959 Eighth Avenue
New York, New York 10019

Copyright © 1975 by Dan Saunders
Published by arrangement with the author

ISBN: 0-380-00471-2

First Avon Printing, September, 1975

AVON TRADEMARK REG. U.S. PAT. OFF. AND
FOREIGN COUNTRIES, REGISTERED TRADEMARK—
MARCA REGISTRADA, HECHO EN CHICAGO, U.S.A.

Printed in the U.S.A.

THIS IS MY ALASKA

1
Tangle with a Moose

My yellow rubber raft drifted slowly with the easy current of Alaska's Big Susitna River. Lying idly back in the raft, I let the challenges of my job slip away under the soothing influence of the warm sunshine and the atmosphere of peace and tranquillity. I observed the riverbanks and the tall, stately white birch and cottonwood trees framed by a backdrop of high, rugged, snowcapped mountains.

Ahead of me, tied to my raft by a twenty-foot rope, drifted a similar raft, occupied by my friend Dick Justin. Lazily, I looked over at Dick and, remembering the day a year ago when I had first met him, grinned. Who'd have thought then we'd be here today, quietly coasting by colonies of busy muskrats and beaver dams under construction. There was nothing noisier in this quiet scene than ducks flapping their wings in flight. Startled by our sudden appearance, they were lifting off the water.

Relaxed and grateful to this new country which was now my home, I absorbed the peace of the moment. It would have been easy to fall asleep.

Through my nearly closed eyes I saw Dick lying back in his raft, hat over his eyes, also appearing to be resting comfortably.

I smiled when I remembered how we met. I had been wandering up and down the concourse of the Seattle-Tacoma Airport, awaiting boarding time on the big Northwest Orient jet that would take me to Anchorage, Alaska, and a new life on the last frontier. The tall, handsome fellow beside me introduced himself as Dick Justin, and said he also was headed for Anchorage.

We went into the airport coffee shop and watched the drizzling rain fall outside the windows as we sipped coffee and got acquainted. I saw the glistening reflection of the white runway lights and blue taxiway lights against the wet blacktop, and I wondered what lay ahead for both of us.

Dick told me he was an aircraft mechanic on his way to a job in Anchorage for a flight service at Merrill Field. I was, I told Dick, on my way to Anchorage to work for the Federal Aviation Agency as an inspector. I had just completed seven years as a police officer in a large midwestern town, plus a tour of duty as a deputy sheriff for Multnomah County at Portland, Oregon.

A lifelong hunger of mine had been to live and work in a vigorous climate. Night work, which prevented daytime sporting activities, had begun to lose its appeal for me.

What I had been doing was rewarding, but not enough. So when the opportunity came for a new life, a new career in what looked like a still-untamed outdoors in the northland, I leaped eagerly at it. The spot with the FAA was too good to pass up. It offered a challenge that, as a trained criminologist, I had subconsciously been moving toward for years.

Since my childhood, I had spent all my spare hours in the woods, hills, and valleys, hunting and camping in the open, loving the clean, free wilderness life. The thought of living in Alaska thrilled me. I dreamed of her deep, silent valleys, unpeopled and still, her lofty mountain ranges, purple canyons and wide rivers—and the call of the wild evoked a strong response in me. My very spirit answered that call. At the airport, Dick and I talked about the chances for making new friends, hunting and fishing trips, adventures we could only imagine at that time. We agreed that we shared an urge to try the northland; we wanted the chance of adventure on that last frontier.

Now on the Big Susitna River, I took another look at Dick. He had turned out to be as ready to adopt Alaska as a permanent home as I was. I was about to lie back and sleep when we drifted around a sharp bend in the river. Suddenly all hell erupted with Dick's frenzied shout: "Hey, you, beat it! Get out of the way!"

I sat upright just in time to see the backside of a big bull moose directly in front of Dick's raft. The big bull turned quickly toward Dick as he swung at it with his paddle, and in the next instant the calm water exploded in a bellowing, shouting, thrashing tangle of legs, moose, raft, equipment, and rifles.

I grabbed frantically for the rope connecting the two rafts, but an instant later felt my own raft turn over as the cold, green water closed over me. When I came thrashing to the surface in water about four feet deep, Dick was standing waist-deep in the water, swinging wildly at the moose, which was trying to thrash its way clear. I heard a splat as Dick connected with his paddle, and then the moose lunged away from Dick, straight toward me. Scrambling furiously for the bank, I tried to get out of its way. The huge bull thundered by me like a PT boat, spraying water in all directions. Dick and I splashed around in the river, collecting rafts and supplies, and crawled out on the bank as wet as two drowned rats and both plenty mad.

Finally, we established ourselves on the bank for a drying-out period. We unpacked our soggy equipment and hung our clothing on bushes to dry in the warm sunshine. We twisted and wrung out our water-logged sleeping bags as mosquitoes buzzed around us in hordes. We were forced to suspend our activities long enough to smear on large quantities of insect repellent.

As he rubbed the stuff on his skin, Dick muttered, "Big deal. Floating along, minding our own business, and that darn moose messing up the whole works."

I said bitterly, "Wish I had that bull's rack to hang up on a wall. That'd even the score a little."

Dick looked at me. I looked at Dick. We both looked and felt so ridiculous after tangling with the moose that we started to laugh.

I couldn't resist making contrasts. "Look at all the items we have with us. They're minimal, and light enough to carry, but enough to keep us going and sustain us comfortably. Do you remember when you said you weren't even bringing long-johns to Alaska? It's been a long year and we've learned a lot since we flew up here a year ago."

"You bet. I'll never forget that flight, either. . . ."

As the Northwest Orient jet rolled away from the terminal in the rain and darkness, we fastened our seat belts. Our eyes, however, were fastened on the beautiful brunette stewardess as she made her welcoming speech and demonstrated the use of the emergency oxygen equipment.

Dick leaned over toward me and whispered, "Get a load of that!"

"I already have," I whispered back.

As the stewardess walked by, we both gave her our brightest smiles; she looked me in the eye and returned a polite but warm smile. I heard Dick grumble beside me: "How come the pretty ones give you the smile, but not me?"

Silent laughter shook me. "It must be my brand of toothpaste."

"Yeah, I'll bet."

At the end of the field the big airplane turned onto the center line of the runway and the low whine of the jet engines rapidly built into a screaming crescendo of full take-off power. I felt the big metal bird rush down the runway and in a few seconds the nose lifted into takeoff position and the runway vibration stopped as we lifted into the air.

The lights of the Seattle and Puget Sound areas soon disappeared in the rain below us as the gleaming airliner continued its climb toward the stars. I held commercial pilot and instrument ratings, but with over two thousand hours' flying time I had never been in the cockpit of a big jet airliner. I wondered what the differences between the instrument panel on this plane and a conventional propeller-driven plane would be. I felt the gentle turn and bank as we picked up what I knew would be a general northwesterly heading.

My mind drifted like a magnetic compass and locked on its own northerly heading as I wondered what kind of life lay ahead for me, what Alaska was really like. I hadn't even taken the time to inquire about the details of life in

Alaska, since all I could think about were the new horizons and new adventures I was heading into.

Dick spoke quietly in his seat next to mine. "I think I'll get some sleep."

"Okay, I'll wake you if anything interesting happens."

It was only natural that my thoughts drifted away to the sunlit pastures of my youth in Missouri. I recalled with real joy my high-school days, when I spent my weekends at a small grass-strip airport. Its row of small single-engine planes were tied down beside the lone hangar, which had been converted from an old barn. I remembered my flight instructor, a big, genial man, a former fighter pilot from World War II, and the patient, confident way he taught me the mysteries of flight. I recalled my eager nervousness on the morning when he climbed out of the Piper Cub and told me "Okay, son, take her around the pattern and make three touch-and-go landings, and just fly as though I were in there talking to you."

The pure spirit-lifting joy of my solo flight still sticks in my mind. That flight was soon followed by cross-country flying, and the day soon came when I proudly received my private pilot's license.

During my early flying days, I worked evenings in a small country print shop, running a job press and linotype to pay for my flying, with the few dollars left over barely providing enough gas for my old Model-A Ford coupe. Now, on my way to Alaska, my thoughts drifted to more recent years. I recalled the frantic activity on the deck of an aircraft carrier in Korean waters, the ear-splitting roar of the Wright Turbo-compound engines on the Douglas Skyraiders, and their powerful performance. I recalled the bone-jarring lurch of the catapult takeoffs and the nerve-grinding approaches to the pitching deck of the carrier when the seas were stormy.

But there was no pleasure in remembering more recent times. My mind still carried indelible pictures of the smiling, trusting faces of three small children, one a toddler of two years, another a boy of four years, and a little girl of six. It wasn't easy that night en route to Alaska to understand it was possible I might never see them again. The memory of the recent divorce drove a spearpoint of anguish through my heart and without the gradual warning, which could bring self-control, my eyes became wet.

The big jet continued its flight toward Alaska. I forced my thoughts into less painful channels, recalling bass fishing trips on the White River in southern Missouri, the happy days of swimming and fishing at the Lake of the Ozarks, and the church summer schools during college at Lake Tanecomo. . . .

The soft voice of the stewardess on the P.A. system roused my attention.

"Ladies and gentlemen, please fasten your seat belts. We are preparing to land at Anchorage. The ground temperature at Anchorage is twenty-eight degrees below zero, so please enter the terminal promptly after we land."

I nudged Dick. "Did you hear that?"

His voice was sleepy. "Good grief, man. I didn't even bring any long-johns."

"Don't feel lonely, buddy. Neither did I."

Now, beside the Big Susitna, our clothes were getting dry.

After taking stock of our food supplies, I realized we had lost all our flour and bacon, so after lengthy discussion we decided to supplement our diet with some fish and ptarmigan, which we found were plentiful along the banks. We both carried big-bore rifles, and I also wore a .44 Magnum Smith & Wesson pistol in a cartridge belt-holster rig. Dick remarked, "If you hit a ptarmigan with that cannon, there won't be enough left to eat."

"Well, buddy, there's only one solution, and that would be to shoot them in the head."

Dick guffawed. "I'll give you a buck for every one you can hit in the head."

By virtue of a little luck and careful marksmanship, I managed to collect seven dollars from Dick in the next two days. I had tried vainly to salvage the roll of film in my 35-mm. camera, but did manage to dry out the camera and reload it with a dry roll I found in the bottom of my pack.

We had made previous arrangements with a pilot of a Cessna 180 at Lake Hood seaplane base to pick us up at the mouth of the river where it emptied into Cook Inlet west of Anchorage. We were looking at our area map and estimating our arrival at Cook Inlet, when we heard a thrashing movement in the brush along the bank of the river just across from us. I looked up and saw a large brown bear standing on its hind legs, surveying us with a surprised look on its face.

"Hold real still, Dick," I whispered. "I want some pictures of this old boy."

Dick had been facing the opposite direction. When I raised my camera, Dick turned his head to see what I had been photographing and I saw his eyes open wide with surprise. He swallowed hard several times as his right hand slowly reached out for his rifle.

Again I was whispering. "Don't shoot unless he charges." I reset the camera for another shot and at the second click of the shutter the giant brownie dropped down on all four legs and ran away from us, crashing and rattling through the underbrush, reminding me of a runaway bulldozer.

After the noise subsided, Dick let out his breath in a long sigh. My hands shook as I reset the camera. Dick said, "That was the biggest darned animal I've ever seen in my life!"

I agreed with him.

Breaking camp on a sandbar on our last day on the river, we stowed our equipment into the two rubber rafts that had served us so well on our eight-day journey. I watched the golden sunrise above the Chugach Range east of Anchorage and looked out across the broad expanse of Cook Inlet and the mouth of the river. The gabble of huge flocks of geese all around us seemed to welcome us to their world of wilderness tranquillity. The mud flats at low tide stretched for many miles to the southeast and southwest, and the sluggish current of the river seemed to put a stop to time itself.

I wished the trip would not end. Here in this great wilderness country, I had found peace of mind and spirit. The dreams of my boyish years were finally being realized in the last frontier of America. I had at long last found a small part of the world that had not been spoiled by the thing called progress.

I knew now for sure that I belonged to Alaska, and that this was my home.

I began to wonder why I had come to Alaska. What was I running from? What was the driving force that prompted my journey to this faraway mystic northland? I looked inward, searching my mind. Since I had previously decided a change of scenery was a must, I also wanted to find adventure and the kind of adventure I sought lay in the wilderness. Since early childhood, I had been deeply intrigued by the mysteries of the tall mountains and peaceful valleys, and I felt very much at home now, floating on the quiet river.

The cool southwest wind carried the smell of the mud flats and the tangy salt air felt good. Far away, to the southwest, Mount Redoubt and Mount Illiamna stood outlined in white against the bright-blue sky, and closer west, Mount Spurr, with its active volcano, rose in brilliant pink. The frequently present plume of white smoke from the volcano lifted high and straight into the cobalt dome of the sky, undisturbed by the calm morning breezes. Far to the south, I saw a glint of silver high in the sky as a jet airliner started its descent for a landing at Anchorage International Airport.

I looked back toward the north, where we had spent the past happy days. Visible in the distance was the mighty Father of Mountains, Mt. McKinley, called "Denali" by the Indians, outlined against the morning sunlight. We floated slowly and quietly at the mouth of the river, waiting for the tide to come in so the Cessna would have enough deep water for a safe landing. I took a compass bearing on Mt. Spurr, and another bearing sight on Mt. Susitna, called the "Sleeping Lady" because of its profile, so we could hold our drift to the center of the river drainage.

After another two hours had passed, I felt the strong pull of the incoming tide and my wristwatch told me the plane was about due. I dug around in my pack and found the old Navy flare pistol and loaded it with a green cartridge. Another thirty minutes passed, and then I heard the drone of a single-engine plane approaching from the direction of Anchorage. About a mile to the southeast, I saw the Cessna and, raising the flare pistol high above my head, I pulled the trigger and heard the boom of the explosion and saw the thin trail of smoke as the flare arced into the sky; then I saw the bright green of the burning flare.

Immediately the wings of the Cessna dipped and banked in our direction. I raised my fly rod straight up with a strip of white gauze bandage tied to its tip so the pilot could estimate the wind direction and speed.

The silver plane with its black-and-yellow stripe banked and circled low above us, rocking the wings. The pilot lowered the flaps, turning into the wind, and we watched the small plane flare into a perfect, smooth landing on its floats. Taxiing up to us, the pilot cut the engine and we climbed onto the floats and started loading equipment into the plane.

Deflating the rafts, we stowed them into the baggage compartment, then climbed into the plane and locked the door. The engine roared back into life and the pilot gunned it into full takeoff power as we rapidly picked up speed and lifted off the water, headed for home.

Again, I looked back to the northwest toward the river we had come to know so intimately. I thought about the moose and bear, and the many beautiful scenes of nature and wildlife we had witnessed on our trip. I longed to be back on the river, but I knew that many happy adventures lay ahead.

2
Hideaway Cabin

My old Ford pickup rattled and bumped over the narrow dirt road that wound through the hills in the north end of the Matanuska Valley, while the warm afternoon sunshine slanted down through the proud groves of white birch trees. Here and there a dark patch of spruce trees crowded through the bright yellow autumn leaves, and, far to the north, I could see the dignified peak of Mt. McKinley outlined against the clear blue sky.

To the west, the summit of Mt. Foraker stood in companion majesty, clearly visible through the more than one hundred miles of mountain air. Jim Boothe, one of my closest friends, rode in the pickup with me as we headed for his homestead cabin back in the hills. We talked as we drove along, planning to begin a moose hunt early the next morning.

We had left Anchorage just after getting off work in order to make the most of a beautiful weekend of hunting, relaxing, and reminiscing. Typical of men on a hunting trip, we let our talk revolve around guns, past hunting trips, outdoor equipment, and cabin building.

Several years earlier, Jim and his wife, Evelyn, had moved to Alaska from Idaho. Now I enjoyed hearing Jim tell of deer, elk, and bear-hunting trips he had made in the rugged Idaho mountains. When we came to the top of a small rise, Jim pointed to a driveway leading off the road to the right.

"Well, we're here."

We swung back into the timber a short distance and in front of us stood a beautiful log cabin, surrounded by a cathedral of white birch trees. The lengthening shadows of the evening sun lit up the scene in calm splendor and an air of quiet solitude surrounded us. Bright yellow leaves fluttered gently in the chilly evening breeze and the grass rustled softly with the passing of the wind. The technicolor of nature's beauty gripped me and I saw the beginning of a fiery Alaskan sunset.

Standing in silence in front of the cabin, I watched as the wild splendor of crimson, gold, pink, and orange spread across the western sky, and I saw the phenomenal band of green in the sky, separating the rainbow of color from the blue dome of heaven. The sky turned dark as we unloaded our rifles and equipment from the pickup.

Inside the cabin, Jim soon had a fire going in the stove and the smell of coffee filled the room. After a light supper we sat around the stove, with our feet up, and the effect of the pleasant surroundings began to sink in. I felt far away from the cares of the world and happy to be in this beautiful cabin deep in the heart of the wilderness.

Walking out in front of the cabin, I looked up at a dark sky filled with glittering stars; to the east, over the dark outline of the trees, a full hunting moon started its climb, taking me back to memories of youthful nights in the hills of Missouri.

There with friends I had chased after a pack of coon hounds. The musical, bawling tenor of a hound on a hot trail still lingered in my mind, and I heard once again the yodel of a big blue-tick hound barking "treed."

I smelled the pungent smoke of many a past campfire and remembered the taste of "hobo" coffee from an old tin cup. I saw once more the big oak trees draped with moss and felt the joy of fatigue from running cross-country after the pack of baying hounds. Here, in a different land and a different time, I thanked the old moon for the happy memories, and listened closely, this time to the yapping of coyotes borne to me on the night wind. Moving back into the cabin, I climbed into my sleeping bag with a feeling of contentment that soon brought sleep.

Jim shook me. I vaguely heard him say, "Hey, roll out. You going to sleep all day?"

We laced our boots in the predawn darkness and soon had breakfast out of the way. Shouldering our packs and picking up our rifles, we left the cabin and headed down through the timber. The deep shadows of night still loomed through the trees and a lighter shade of gray showed where Jim had cleared land for earlier planting. Ghostly layers and wisps of ground fog hung across the clearing and under the trees like regiments of departed souls.

Jim walked ahead of me with the silent, easy movement of a born outdoorsman, watchful and alert. We went past the clearing and down into a grove of spruce trees, watching the shadows for signs of movement. The sky to the east began to pale with the first light of dawn and the layers of fog lifted slowly through the trees.

Several yards farther, Jim stopped suddenly, pointing to some dark shadows among the trees. I slipped my binoculars from under my coat and studied the dark forms. Through the powerful glasses I clearly saw the outlines of three moose, and I held up three fingers. Jim nodded.

Slowly, step by step, we moved closer and the only sign of movement from the moose was the back-and-forth twitching of their ears as they eyed us warily. We stopped again, and the glasses showed the animals sharp and clear.

I whispered, "They are all cows."

Jim nodded. "Wherever the cows are, we will probably find a bull or two."

We moved slowly forward, and the three moose disappeared through the trees without a sound. The shadows continued to lift as we walked on down a small canyon and crossed a creek. Ahead of us lay a small pasture, nestled between two ridges, and the grass on the pasture floor looked white with its covering of frost. Jim motioned me to move down the left side of the pasture, while he worked the right side.

We moved slowly out into the edges of the pasture, watching each other for signs while studying the groves of trees and underbrush at the sides. About halfway across the pasture, I saw him stop and I halted to watch him. He stood frozen for a moment, then raised his rifle slowly, looking through the sights. A few seconds later, the rolling boom of his .300 Magnum echoed across the clearing and bounced off the hills.

I heard the click of the bolt on his rifle as he snapped another cartridge into the chamber, and stood with his rifle at the ready. After a few moments, Jim motioned me to move over to him. I swung across the pasture, easing a cartridge into the chamber of my own rifle. We walked forward to where a large, dark-brown shape lay at the edge of the pasture. A big bull moose lay on his side, unmoving in death.

Jim spoke. "Stand fast for a few minutes and let's make sure he doesn't get up and charge."

"What do you think he weighs?"

"I don't know for sure, but he is a little larger than average, so will probably go over twelve hundred pounds."

I eased around the big animal, coming up behind it, while Jim held his sights just behind the bull's ear. Moving clear of Jim's sighting area, I reached out with the barrel of my rifle and poked the animal, but saw no signs of life. Looking closer, I saw where Jim's single bullet had struck behind the left ear, killing the moose instantly. I congratulated Jim, commenting on the spot at which the bullet had hit.

Jim grinned and said, "Well, that's where I aimed."

We removed the shells from the rifle chambers, reloaded the magazines, then began the job of butchering the animal. We shed our coats and rolled up our sleeves. Jim showed me how to cut the carcass, clean the animal, and peel the hide. Then came the chore of packing the meat and antlers. Tying a front quarter onto my packboard, I grunted with surprise at the massive weight of the meat.

Jim smiled knowingly. "Those front quarters will weigh nearly two hundred pounds each, and we will need to make two trips to finish the job."

I groaned inwardly, feeling the weight of the pack straps bite into my shoulders. Starting the one-mile trip back to the cabin, we moved steadily and the sweat streamed down my face. I soon learned the art of balancing my own weight on the packboard and the back-breaking chore became a little easier—but the load became heavier with each foot of ground covered.

When the cabin came into view, I heaved a sigh of relief. After unloading the pack, I felt as if I were floating a foot above the ground. We sat down and drank a well-earned cup of coffee, resting for the return trip. While we talked, I looked up and saw a cow moose standing in the driveway, not over seventy-five yards away.

"Why couldn't that darned animal have horns on it!"

Jim was amused. "Keep your eyes open. They're all around here."

We returned to the bull moose and loaded the rear quarters and the remaining meat. The last trip back to the cabin seemed easier than the first, and my sore muscles loosened to the task.

After wrapping the meat in cloth bags, Jim fired up the stove, and the smell of fresh moose liver and onions soon filled the cabin. We ate a hearty meal. Then we sat on the front porch of the cabin and watched the beginning of another beautiful sunset. A porcupine waddled across the front yard in haughty dignity, and we both laughed at his ponderous gait.

The afterglow of the thrilling sunset soon brought the chill of evening. With darkness moving in silently, we went inside the cabin to continue our conversation seated around the stove and, later, to enjoy another dinner of liver and onions.

Finally, I got up from my chair by the stove to go out the back door; after taking two steps out the door, I saw the shadow of a bull moose standing in the driveway not thirty yards from the cabin. I eased back inside the cabin, grabbed my rifle, and started again for the back door.

I watched Jim as a smile spread over his face. "What did you see, a shadow with horns?"

"You're darn right I did, and he's right outside the back door."

I eased back out into the darkness to look for the moose and heard a snort and the thunder of hooves coming straight at me. I couldn't see the animal, but I could sense his high-speed charge, and I leaped for the back door of the cabin. I hooked the toe of my boot on the threshold of the door and sprawled full-length into the cabin as the echoes of the departing moose faded away.

Jim kidded me as I got up from the floor.

"What are you trying to do, sucker him into the cabin, then shoot him?"

"That darn fool tried to run me down!"

Jim shook with laughter and finally managed to answer, "Well, they sure won't wait around for you."

I crawled into my sleeping bag that night, my mind filled with all sorts of evil ways to kill moose.

The next morning, with breakfast finished, we loaded the moose meat into the pickup and cleaned up the cabin. Walking out to the pickup, I happened to look back toward the clearing and see another bull moose standing there, not two hundred yards away.

Jim looked at the moose. "He's all yours."

I lifted my rifle from the pickup, took careful aim at the neck just in front of the shoulders, felt the bucking recoil, and heard the crack of the shot. The bullet smacked home and the bull dropped in his tracks.

I turned to Jim. "Well, let's get started all over again."

We took our packs to where the animal lay, and soon had another load of moose meat added to the pickup.

When we were finished, Jim locked the cabin door and we climbed into the cab of the pickup. Before starting the engine, I looked longingly at the beautiful little cabin tucked away in the trees and commented, "A real hideway cabin."

As we rolled down the road toward home, Jim finally spoke. "And it's about time you started looking for a place to build yourself a cabin."

I thought about this for a while. And I decided that cabin-building fever had hit me.

3
Cabin-Building Fever

Steaming coffee tasted good as I sat in a booth at Peggy's Airport Cafe and watched the quiet snow falling outside the window. This was the beginning of my second winter in Alaska and the time had come to decide whether or not this state was really to be my home—or whether there was any reason for me to return south.

I thought of the several friends I had made since coming here and I thought, too, of the many experiences I had already enjoyed. Something stuck in my mind, something I couldn't quite put my finger on, but I knew I had fallen in love with this wide-open, rugged land.

I had come to treasure the friendly, easy way of the Alaskan, his frank openness in dealing with people, and the mutual trust and respect that men of the frontier held for each other. I had camped in the lonely wilderness, fished the rivers and streams and hunted the bear and moose, and a deep sense of belonging held me.

I recalled the big cities I had left, their milling mobs of people, the rush and roar of traffic, the frantic way of life, and, at this hour, I made my decision. I knew I would never be satisfied with the old way of life. The call of the wilderness grew stronger by the moment. I sensed a challenge, a new opportunity to be what I wanted to be, part of a new land, a new frontier yet to be explored, and I knew now I could make of myself whatever I wished to be.

Here was my home; here I would live and die. I accept-

21

ed the silent challenge with a glad heart, ready and willing to take what Alaska had to offer and make the most of it. I wanted to be a part of her, to learn her secret ways, to live with the land; somehow I knew for sure the reward would be great.

Looking back over the past two months, I recalled with pleasure the visits I had made to Jim Boothe's cabin, and the urge came over me to build my own cabin. Maybe Jim's idea had caught fire.

The next day at work, I mentioned to Bob Lindgren that I wanted to build a cabin of my own but had no idea where to look for a small tract of land that would match my budget and suit my purpose. Bob said he knew a man who lived back in the mountains near the town of Willow who might be willing to sell ten acres for a reasonable price, so we made plans to drive up past Willow on a Saturday and see what could be arranged.

I immediately headed for the library and checked out two or three books on cabin-building and soon began to digest ideas and different methods of log-cabin construction. The remainder of that week, I pestered all the old-timers I knew, asking them about the different methods of raising a cabin, and by Saturday I had an idea of what I wanted.

Early Saturday morning, Bob and I headed up the highway. Bob had built a cabin of spruce logs just three years earlier, and he filled my head with the do's and don'ts of working with logs. I had helped build two frame houses in the past and had a general notion of house-building, but I was learning that there was a vast difference between building a frame structure and a log house.

Driving through the town of Willow, we turned onto a gravel road that wound back into the mountains and later crossed Hatcher Pass. The road began to climb higher and higher into the Talkeetna Mountains, and we finally turned into a rough dirt driveway to wind our way back through groves of birch and spruce trees. Around a bend in the driveway, I saw a snug log cabin with smoke coming from its chimney. The quiet solitude of winter and white snow told me this was the way of life I had been searching for.

A tall redheaded man came from the cabin and greeted

Bob. Soon we were seated inside the cabin, drinking hot coffee. I had long ago learned that the coffeepot is a definite part of Alaskan hospitality, and the common greeting among Alaskans is "Come on in and have a cup of coffee."

The three of us were soon close friends. When I explained the purpose of my visit, our host said, "Well, I've got ten acres I'll sell. Let's walk down through the timber and I'll show you where it lies."

The three of us walked quietly through a classic winter wonderland of spruce trees white with new-fallen snow. I saw countless tracks of ptarmigan, moose and wolf, and one set of tracks made by a late-hibernating bear.

After we had crossed a frozen stream and walked up a small rise, the tall woodsman said, "Here is the corner marker of the ten acres. Let's walk the perimeter."

As we wandered down the survey line, I decided this was it. I had found what I wanted. I thought of my limited savings and worried about whether or not the price would fit my budget. I returned to the starting stake and turned to the tall redhead to ask what this would cost.

He thought awhile and when quoted a price I felt a surge of elation. My savings would cover the cost with a little left over.

I spoke quickly. "I'll take it."

We shook hands on the deal and I wrote a check for earnest money and then made arrangements to meet him at the bank the following week to close the deal. Four days later, I was the happy owner of ten acres of the most beautiful wilderness forest I had ever seen.

The first problem facing me was clearing trees for a driveway and the cabin site. I decided I would cut only what trees were actually necessary for building the cabin. I shopped around Anchorage and bought a used chain saw with an extra chain, and the project got under way.

Each weekend I left Anchorage in my old Ford pickup, loaded with food supplies, chain saw, axes, tools, and sleeping bag. I had set up a ten-by-twelve-foot wall tent as my "construction headquarters" and my weekend and holiday home.

The Coleman lantern and stove became a way of life; the hard work of felling the spruce trees and peeling them into cabin logs also took off excess weight and inches from my waistline. I felt a sense of satisfaction as I watched the pile of logs grow and had a personal pride in my efforts.

I looked forward to the weekend and waited impatiently for the snarling roar of the chain saw and the solid bite of a sharp ax into the logs. The pile of logs, spaced with branches for drying, seemed to grow with agonizing slowness. The sea of stumps in the clearing kept reminding me of more hard work ahead. I enjoyed working in the clear, cold mountain air. Each day the winter sun lit up my world of white with a rare beauty.

During the coldest part of the winter, the months of January and February, a cow moose came to watch me. The noise of the saw seemed to interest her and I talked to her as I worked. We had a mutual agreement to keep at least thirty feet between us, and, on occasion, I detoured around her as she nibbled at the willow branches growing along the creek. Several times, I saw her with three or four other cows and after watching the movements and tracks of the moose, I decided I was homesteading right in the middle of their winter camping grounds.

One bitter cold morning I rolled out of my sleeping bag, got a fire going, and had just put the coffeepot on the Coleman stove when a commotion broke out down at the creek. With all the snarling, snapping, and thrashing in the underbrush, I felt it would be a good idea to take my rifle along and, strapping on my snowshoes, I headed for the uproar.

Topping a rise, I saw a pack of five wolves circling around my friend, the old cow moose. She had backed into a clump of willows and was facing her tormentors with real determination, her ears laid back, hackles up, and her razor-sharp front hooves ready to strike. Looking behind her, I saw one of the wolves had caught her by the left hamstring, and a quick shot from my rifle dropped him in his tracks. At the blast of the rifle, the remainder of the pack scattered through the underbrush, disappearing in seconds. The moose limped off down the creek and I soon had the wolf hide stretched on a frame to dry.

Winter turned to spring and the roads into their usual muddy quagmire. I soon found the Ford pickup was useless in the deep mud. On the advice of several friends and neighbors, I traded off the old Ford for an ex-military Dodge Power Wagon with four-wheel drive and a winch on the front bumper. With some painting and minor repairs, the Dodge looked equal to the task of cabin-building. I soon learned the value of the four-wheel drive and the winch.

Many wet, rainy mornings, the winch pulled me out of the mud and got me on my way. I also learned to chain the rear of the Dodge to a tree and use the winch to pull stumps out of the ground. My neighbor had a D-6 Caterpillar bulldozer, and after we had become acquainted he offered to let me use the dozer if I would pay for the diesel fuel. This turned out to be a real blessing; after two weekends of running the big cat, I had a gravel road into the cabin and the cabin site cleared, ready for actual construction to start.

On the following weekend, an inspiration seized me. I stood looking at the back edge of the ten acres and I decided the area was a perfect location for a landing strip for my Piper Cub. I climbed back on the bulldozer and soon had a strip cleared with plenty of room for landing and take off.

The pile of peeled logs continued to grow as spring turned to summer. While the logs lay seasoning in the warm sun, I began the task of digging footings for the cabin. By using native rocks and hand-mixed concrete, I soon had the footings in. Then I sat back for a breathing spell and decided to catch up on my fishing and hunting.

Memorial Day came with its three-day vacation and I loaded my sleeping bag and fly rod into the Piper Cub and took off for the Copper River country. I knew of a wide stretch of gravel bar where the salmon fishing was good; before long I had the Cub tied down to some boulders and a camp set up nearby.

The three days were filled with glorious sunrises and sunsets and evenings by the campfire. A hike of one mile brought me to a small lake where the rainbow trout and grayling were striking at every fly I tied on my line. It didn't take long to get my fill of fish and I laughed at the antics of a black bear and her twin cubs. They reminded me of children at play, with their wrestling, chasing each other, fighting and squalling, just like two kids. The evening of the third day arrived all too soon, and I lifted off the gravel bar to head the Cub back towards Anchorage.

When the ground around the cabin site had dried sufficiently, I decided to fly into the strip at the cabin in order to save travel time between the cabin and Anchorage. Having taken off from Merrill Field, I was soon over the site and turned into the wind, lined up for the strip. As the Cub began to settle down, I looked toward the far end of the strip and saw a cow moose wander out into my way, followed by a wobbly legged calf. I shoved the throttle open and lifted away from the strip.

Climbing back up several hundred feet, I circled for five minutes while the cow and her calf decided to wander off into the brush. I watched closely until she had moved away from the strip, then I flared out and completed my landing. Following several weekends of flying to my homestead, I appreciated the thirty-minute flight as compared to the two and one half hours' driving. Flying in and out of the dirt strip gave me several practical lessons in cross-wind landings and takeoffs.

One Sunday evening a severe gust of cross-wind hit the Cub as I was taking off. I held my breath as the tips of the spruce and birch trees whispered gently under the right wingtip and the engine thundered its song of full power.

Crabbing into the wind, the Cub won out in the battle for altitude. I breathed easier as the altimeter continued its climb.

During this first summer of flying into the dirt strip I learned how much load the Cub could safely handle and I checked carefully on every trip to insure against overloading. The steady, reliable performance of the Cub satisfied me in every way and I understood that dependability and economy had more appeal for me than the fast planes with their gas-consuming, high-performance engines. The warm, happy summer passed into autumn and the leaves of birch and cottonwood trees turned bright yellow. The cabin-building progressed, and I figured that, by the next spring, the logs would have seasoned sufficiently. So I concentrated the remaining fall weekends on stockpiling all the odds and ends that would be needed when the actual cabin-raising began.

Early one frosty autumn morning, I flew toward the homestead and saw snow on the peaks of the Talkeetna Range. I knew that before long the Cub would be wearing skis instead of wheels. The angle of the sun above the horizon slid further toward the southeast with each succeeding morning and the shadows lengthened each evening.

On this particular morning, I swung over my nearest neighbor's cabin and was startled to see him lying on the ground near his woodpile. I circled for a closer look, but he never moved. Then I saw the spreading stain of red near his right foot. I immediately kicked the Cub into a hard forward slip, cutting power for a fast landing, and ran the half mile up the survey line to my neighbor's place.

I found him alive, but weak from loss of blood. The head had come off his ax while he was chopping wood, inflicting a ghastly wound on his right instep. I pulled off his boot, stripped off my undershirt, and wound a tight bandage around the wound, then pulled my belt up tight near his groin to stop the flow of blood.

Hoisting the tall redhead onto my shoulders, I dogtrotted back to the plane, fear eating into me at every step. I loaded him into the back seat of the Cub and quickly had the engine roaring at full throttle for takeoff. Climbing out above the trees, I turned for Anchorage and started calling for help on the plane radio.

The FAA station at Talkeetna answered, and I told the operator to advise Merrill Field that I had a badly injured passenger and that I requested an ambulance to stand by. Talkeetna relayed my message and then called me, saying the ambulance would be waiting.

Within a few minutes, I was within radio range of Merrill Field and was cleared for a straight-in approach. I greased the plane onto the runway and saw the Fire Department ambulance chasing me down the runway. I turned off onto a taxiway and stopped; we soon had the injured man loaded into the ambulance. I parked the plane, got into my pickup, and headed for the Providence Hospital, which at that time was at Ninth and "L" Streets.

After two hours of waiting, I was told by the doctor that my neighbor was okay, but would be hospitalized for a few days. It had been, the doctor said, a close shave.

Once again, I silently thanked the rugged, dependable engine in the Cub.

Within a few weeks I had the floor joists, mud sills, and fireplace completed. The golden days of autumn were filled with Nature's splendor; the fiery sunsets thrilled me, day after day. Soon the first snows of winter fell and I halted the cabin project until the coming of spring.

I relaxed and enjoyed the beauty of the wilderness around me; I watched the ptarmigan and snowshoe rabbit as they changed into their winter dress of white. The beaver and muskrat worked busily in the lakes and streams, preparing for the hard freeze that was not far off. The haunting cry of the loon became more plaintive, and the honking of geese at night told of flights headed south.

I watched a big grizzly high on a mountainside search restlessly for a winter den and I saw signs of black bear moving into the canyons for their annual winter denning. Ice formed along the edges of the creek and the nearby small lake; soon the ducks and geese were gone. I watched the loon family that had summered at the lake take off one morning. I knew from the way they climbed into the sky that this was their final flight for the season.

The ground grew hard with frost as the big freeze settled in and the land lay locked tight in the grip of Arctic winter. As the snow deepened around the cabin site, the silence became more profound. By this time I had removed the wheels from the Cub and replaced them with skis. A busy work schedule that included a heavy travel itinerary kept me away from the homestead for several weeks, but the time came when the air filled with the sights and sounds of the Christmas season.

This was the time to be merry and rejoice, but the bitter memory of the loss of three small children ate into me. Once again, I turned for comfort to the wilderness. While all the town was busy with plans for the holiday season, I thought of the tent standing at the cabin site and I yearned more than ever to be alone—to commune with the Great Creator and feel the healing power of the wilderness silence.

On Christmas Eve I filled the gas tanks of the Cub and took off at noon for the cabin. Flying low over the area, I saw only the tracks of the moose and wolf and the snowshoe rabbit as I turned the Cub into the final approach and let the skis settle onto the snow of the runway. Having tied the plane down, I strapped on my snowshoes and walked to the cabin site. There I found everything as I had left it, marked only by the tracks of the wilderness creatures.

Within a few minutes I had a fire roaring in the Yukon stove in the tent and I settled in for a week of peace and quiet. I had taken the battery and the motor oil out of the plane and put them beside the stove, where they would be ready when I wanted to leave.

At this time of year the sun rose in the southeast around 10:30 A.M. and slid across the southern skyline, lingered briefly on the horizon, then disappeared around 2:30 P.M. The sky to the southwest would glow with the gold and crimson of a wild Alaskan sunset, then the silent dark of an Arctic night would take over.

I spent the long evenings of the Christmas holidays reading by the light of the gas lantern; the poems of Tennyson, Whitman, and Riley became my close companions. I spent many night hours pouring over the Bible, and found comfort in the great mysteries of the Scriptures.

During the brief daylight hours, I walked the silent, white trails of the moose and caribou, and followed the busy life of the ptarmigan and field mice and the myriad tracks of the snowshoe rabbit that led to nowhere.

On the third night of my vacation, the clouds drifted away and the stars shone in all their brilliant beauty, stretched from one edge of the night sky to the other. A bright glow in the eastern sky told of an early moonrise; within an hour the night world was bathed in a soft, blue-white moonglow.

I looked deep into the dark shadows and saw the darker shadow of an occasional moose move slowly through the night. I heard the now-familiar howl of the wolf, quavering its clear tenor through the canyon and nearby valley. This song of the wild gripped me in a strong way and dug itself deep into my subconscious. Looking at the full moon riding in the dark Arctic sky, I understood the urge of the wolf to pour out his wild song.

The stirring, quiet beauty of the night gradually

restored my desire for life and a new satisfaction with my surroundings took over.

On the last morning of my winter vacation I put a canvas hood over the engine cowling of the plane and fired up the Herman Nelson heater to heat the engine. Then came a three-hour session of preheating the engine. After that, I poured in the hot oil, connected the battery cables, then crossed my fingers. A few seconds of growling protest from the starter brought a welcome roar from the engine. Following warmup I took off and circled the clearing and the north woods Shangri-La soon slid out of sight under my left wing. I had wished my stay in the wilderness might continue, but though it had ended temporarily I was able now to return to work with a new outlook on life—and begin the restless wait for the arrival of warmer weather.

The passing of winter brought the melting of snow and the nights were soon filled with gabbling and honking as flights of ducks and geese returned. Before the creeks and rivers filled with the spring runoff, I had the logs notched and cut to size and, finally, the walls of my cabin began to rise. The completed door and window frames were set into place, and I began to struggle with the logs in a sea of mud as the ground softened in the thaw.

Again, the winch on the Dodge came into play, skidding the logs up and into place. I heaved a sigh of relief as I thought of the many hours of toil the machine had saved me. By the time the ground had dried in the heat of the sun and the long summer days, I had the walls finished and the spruce rafters and ridge pole in place. I nailed the roughsawn planks on the rafters, then applied two coats of roll roofing as a prelude to a session of hot tar mopping to make the roof weathertight. The following three weekends were spent in endless chinking of all the cracks between and around the logs. My hands and arms itched from handling the fiberglass strips of insulation.

At last my project stood completed; the oil-coated logs shone in the sun and a great feeling of happiness filled me. My neighbor, the tall redhead, came down and looked the cabin over carefully.

"By golly, it looks mighty good to me."

We held a housewarming right there on the spot and celebrated by building the first fire in the fireplace and boiling a pot of coffee. We sat on rough chairs made out of spruce poles and talked of pleasant things like hunting and fishing and the joy and satisfaction of seeing the results of many months' toil and labor.

Then came a dinner of moose steaks, dandelion greens, and canned peaches, after which we sat around the fireplace and talked far into the night. The warm glow of satisfaction and pride stayed with me as I crawled into my sleeping bag on the handhewn spruce bunk.

Now that the cabin was completed, I spent the next several weeks traveling around Alaska performing my duties with the FAA; I also told my good friend Jack Jefford, senior pilot of the FAA in Alaska, of the completion of my cabin project.

Jack smiled in his easy way. "So it looks like you're here to stay, all right."

4

Ghosts around
the Campfire

The Friday morning office routine started off with a bang, and the thought of the monthly report deadlines lying on my desk didn't help my disposition. After having worked for the Federal Aviation Agency for over a year as an inspector, I was looking forward to my annual vacation which started the next day, but only if I got those reports finished on time.

The phone on my desk rang. The cheerful voice of Ed Wardley boomed into my ear. "Well, buddy, what have you planned for your vacation?"

I growled. "Nothing. You got any bright ideas?"

He chuckled. "I sure have. Meet me at Peggy's Cafe for lunch. I've got something too good to pass up."

Ed Wardley was a pilot for a small bush feeder airline working in and around Anchorage and the interior of Alaska. His knowledge of the wilderness and the mountains would fill several big city telephone directories. I had met Ed shortly after I came to Alaska, when we had both become storm bound in the village of Talkeetna. Talking to those who knew Ed, I found his skill as a pilot and woodsman was legendary.

While we ate a light lunch at Peggy's Cafe near the Merrill Field Airport, Ed outlined plans for a Dall sheep-hunting trip high into the Wrangell Mountains in the eastern part of Alaska. The Wrangell Mountains are known for high and rugged peaks, glaciers and canyons, and terrain never before having known the footprint of man.

I worried a little about the possibility of becoming lost or injured high in the lofty, sun-shadowed range, but Ed explained the situation.

"I have a close friend who is an Athabascan Indian and he has spent most of his life in that part of the country. He wants to go along, so I don't see how we could miss."

I had a lot of faith in Ed's ability and judgment, and I knew of the uncanny wilderness knowledge of the Athabascan Indians. So I agreed.

"Okay, let's leave as soon as we can get our equipment ready, say noon tomorrow?"

Ed cracked his big grin. "Good deal. I'll pick you up at noon tomorrow and we'll fly to Gulkana airport and then take a four-wheel drive pickup from there. We can haul a weasel on a trailer for use when the going gets rough."

I worked frantically for the remainder of the afternoon to get my reports done. I was driven by the prospects of a challenging hunting trip into some of the most beautiful and rugged mountains in the world. Between reports, I made hurried notes about the pieces of equipment I would take on the trip. Groceries didn't bother me, since Ed had agreed to bring them and we could split the cost.

Late that evening I called Ed on the telephone and we checked over the items on our lists, eliminating everything except those necessary for roughing it in the mountains.

On the following day, high noon found us in Ed's Cessna 180 at Merrill Field, the engine warming up as we went over the check list and preflight routines. With clearance from the tower, the soft rumble of the engine on the 180 burst into a howl of power as Ed opened the throttle for takeoff. The bright sunshine warmed the inside of the cockpit as we climbed on a northeasterly heading, flying alongside the Chugach Mountains, passing over the town of Palmer, and heading for Chickaloon Pass in the Talkeetna Mountains.

I watched the endless mountain peaks pass by under the wings as we continued toward Gulkana and the power song of the engine lifted my spirits in anticipation of the adventures that lay ahead. The runway of the Gulkana airport soon came into view and the voice of the FAA controller at Gulkana crackled into the cabin loudspeaker, clearing us to land.

The Cessna eased onto the runway under Ed's skillful guidance and we soon rolled to a stop on the parking apron at the edge of the taxiway and tiedown area.

Off to the side of the parking apron was a blue four-wheel-drive Ford pickup, with a man sitting behind its wheel watching us. As the propeller stopped turning, the pickup drove over to our plane and an Indian got out of the cab and walked over. Ed introduced him as John Little Bear, our hunting companion. The grip of his handshake was strong and sincere, and the smile on his face failed to hide the dark, watchful eyes as he looked me over. He glanced at my pack and rifle as I took them from the plane, then turned to Ed.

"Looks like we're going to have a good hunting trip. The weather is good in the Nabesna area, the weasel is running okay, and I like the looks of your friend."

Ed turned to me with a laugh. "That is one long speech coming from him."

John and I both laughed and I took an immediate liking to this short, stocky, broad-shouldered man; his ready smile and direct but friendly way of speaking created an air of quiet confidence. I soon found he spoke only when necessary, but the wide smile came easily to his face and his dark eyes turned toward the noble peaks of the Wrangell Range, standing purple, silent, and snowcapped in the distance. I gazed at the distant peaks, watching the small clouds that drifted among them, and their shadows that dropped deep into canyons and across the ageless blue glaciers. A strong thrill ran through me. I felt very fortunate to be able to hunt the great Dall sheep with two of the most capable woodsmen and mountaineers in Alaska.

We piled our equipment into the back of the pickup and started up the highway toward Chistochina Lodge, where we were to pick up the trailer and the weasel, a tracked vehicle capable of travel over rough terrain. We drove in silence most of the way, but occasional conversation came easily as though we had known each other for years. I asked John where he lived.

His answer was this: "On the highway close to Delta

Junction. My people are Athabascan and have lived in and around this part of the state for many, many years. I can remember my father and grandfather telling of the Klondike gold rush, and how the stampede of miners in the mountains resulted in the death of many of their numbers, due to exposure, frostbite, and a general lack of know-how for mountain living."

In talking with John, I could sense his fierce pride in his tribal ancestry. In one of his apparently rare talking moods, he told me some of the history of the Athabascan (sometimes spelled Athapascan) people, their bouts with sickness, long winters of starvation, wars with neighboring Indian tribes, and some of the folklore handed down from father to son.

He spoke of the ancient tribal rituals of young men reaching manhood, of marriage customs of the long ago, or of the "old ones," as John put it. He also spoke of the coming of the first white men in this area, the fur trappers and prospectors who arrived sometime before the Klondike gold rush, and how they brought the dreaded social diseases into the tribes. His voice deepened and he spoke more slowly.

"My grandfather told me that some of the white men of long ago were good men and some of them were very bad men, treating the old people as though they were slaves."

He turned to me with a smile. "I don't hold any hard feelings toward the white man at all, since my father told me of the teachings of the Bible, where we are to love each other as brothers, and this is the way I feel."

He spoke again. "Some of the customs of my people seemed strange to the first white men, but some of their customs seemed strange to my people, too. Times have changed much even since I was a small boy, but we live more like the white man in this day."

I sat deep in thought. My respect for this mountain man increased with each hour that passed. When he looked at the faraway mountain peaks, his eyes took on a distant gaze and in my imagination I could see his ancestors camped in the valleys, the children and women around the wickiups, the smoke of the campfires lifting into the glow of the sunsets, the countless flocks of ducks and geese on the marshes. I could feel a deep sense of empathy with John and his ancestors, and I wished I could have stood beside the campfires of "the old ones" and heard their songs and watched the ceremonial dances.

We pulled into Chistochina Lodge, where we hooked up the trailer carrying the weasel, then filled the gas tanks and ate a brief lunch. After lunch we spread a Geodetic Survey sectional map on the hood of the pickup and I listened with rapt attention as Ed and John, both intimately familiar with the mountains above Nabesna village, discussed the canyons and crags and the locations where the largest concentrations of Dall sheep were known to be. Through quiet conversation the location of our base camp was decided on. I tried to memorize all the features shown on the map, and then took compass bearings from the map to keep in my mind.

I looked around at John and saw a big grin on his face as he watched me; I also heard Ed's deep chuckle.

"He believes in instrument flying, even when he's on the ground."

John spoke with a laugh. "I don't need a compass, but if you paleface boys carry one I don't suppose it will hurt anything."

We all took this as an hilarious joke. Rechecking our equipment, we drove back down the highway to the Nabesna road, which I could see stretching some forty or fifty miles to the southeast into the foothills of the Wrangells. Compared to driving on the blacktop highway, the dusty, gravel Nabesna road was rough and unpleasant, but John kept up the steady forty-mile-per-hour speed that seemed to eat up the distance. Conversation died to a minimum and I watched the long rays of the afternoon sun stretching across the valley. The magnificent crags of the mountains ahead stood out in brilliant white relief against the blue sky. I could feel the engine of the pickup work harder as the road climbed toward the mountains, which by now were growing larger and closer.

The sun continued its descent toward the jagged row of mountain peaks to the west and the snow-capped peaks towering over us turned a soft rose pink, then a deeper pink, and finally a deep lavender. The shadows in the mountains lengthened and the canyons turned a deep purple. The western sky was filled with the wild, awe-inspiring spectrum of an Alaskan sunset.

We drove in silence, each wrapped in his own secret thoughts and dreams. Shortly, there was a bend in the road and we came into the remains of the old Nabesna village. John spoke now. "Only a few people live here now, since the mines have shut down."

I could see the rusted, aging remains of mining activities just past the village, evidence that man had dug here in his endless search for mineral riches. We drove slowly through the village, John and Ed waving to the few faces that showed up at the windows of the old, weatherbeaten houses.

Ed suggested, "Why don't we drive on up to the end of the road and make camp tonight?"

John nodded his approval.

I agreed. "Sounds fine to me."

We soon had a campfire going and our sleeping bags unrolled. I helped Ed as we prepared a simple supper of beans and cold cornbread with fresh coffee from the blackened, battered old coffeepot.

The darkness had crept in around us and a blanket of stillness covered the high end of the valley where we had bedded down. Crags towered over us in the night sky, seeming to offer their friendly protection. The only sounds I could hear were the soft, sighing night winds and the faraway yapping of coyotes. Ed and I spoke occasionally, discussing the merits of different hunting rifles, but John became quiet and took no part in our conversation.

As the fire died down, John rose to his feet and walked to the edge of the circle of firelight, where he stood gazing to the northwest as though straining to see something through the velvet darkness. He stood like that for a full ten minutes without moving or speaking. I looked at Ed with a silent question on my face.

Ed looked at me for a moment before saying quietly, "Something on your mind, John?"

John hesitated a long minute before he answered. "Don't know. I guess not."

He turned slowly and walked back, then sat down and pulled off his boots and rolled up his jacket for a pillow.

Without speaking, he crawled into his sleeping bag and immediately closed his eyes. Ed and I continued to sit, gazing into the fire; I heard the faraway howl of a hunting wolf, echoing the eternal call of the wild.

Suddenly John sat bolt upright in his sleeping bag and gazed again toward the northeast. I began to worry.

Ed asked again: "John, is something bothering you?"

John just shook his head and lay back in his sleeping bag and closed his eyes. Soon Ed and I were fast asleep in our sleeping bags, and the soft night closed gently in around us. . . .

I felt someone shake me. Rolling over, I saw Ed crouched beside me. "Rise and shine, old buddy. Time to roll out."

I saw the dawn creeping across the valley and felt the cold winds of morning. The clear sky promised a good day to hunt. John was already up, rolling his sleeping bag.

"Good morning, you two!" I said.

John looked over at me and again came the big smile and a pleasant good morning. I wondered about his actions of the night before, but then dismissed them from my mind. I rolled my sleeping bag and began to work on a hot breakfast of bacon and flapjacks. With our stomachs full, the day looked brighter and we quickly broke camp.

"I think," Ed began, "we can go a little further with the pickup, so why don't we give it a try?"

John only grunted, but he climbed into the pickup and started the engine without comment. We drove slowly over the rough, rutted old wagon trail; John shifted gears back and forth as the grade increased. We covered about three miles back into a long canyon. John drove the pickup onto a level place, and, without speaking, locked the brakes and got out of the cab.

Ed, in his usual cheerful drawl, said he was ready to work. "Let's get that weasel unloaded and see how far we can go with it."

I walked to the back of the trailer and started removing the tie-down chains, while Ed worked on the front chains. He removed the chains and blocks and climbed into the cab of the weasel. He started the engine and slowly backed it off the tilting trailer and onto the ground.

While the engine idled in warmup, John and I loaded our small amount of equipment into the weasel. I tried several times to engage John in conversation, but he remained silent and answered only when spoken to.

Ed called to me: "Say, have you ever driven a weasel?"

"Look, I don't even know which end of that thing is forward."

"Well, pal, here is where you learn. Get yourself up in the driver's seat."

I climbed into the seat and found two levers where the steering wheel should have been. Ed pointed out the brake pedal, the accelerator, and engine gauges. "Have you ever run a bulldozer?"

"Sure, several times."

"Okay, let 'er rip; I'll show you the trail."

I gunned the engine and we started off with a lurch. I heard John mumble something about a "hotrod," but I soon got the feel of the steering levers as we made our way up the incline of the canyon floor. After about two miles of climbing over rough ground, rocks, and logs, we came to a creek and I looked at the fast-flowing water and braked to a stop. Ed got out and walked up and down the creek bank, then picked up a stick and probed the creek bottom.

He came back and crawled into the weasel.

"Looks like good rock bottom all the way across. Head into that shallow bank and take it slow, but keep power on all the way across."

I dropped into low gear, eased down into the water, and felt the tracks bite into solid rock as we wallowed slowly but steadily across the creek and up the far bank. Two miles of hard climbing later, the steep terrain became rougher and I saw several shale and talus slides above and ahead.

Ed turned toward John. "What do you think, John? Should we pack on in from here?"

John nodded without speaking, and again I wondered why he was so silent this morning, when yesterday he had been more talkative and seemed in a better mood. We unloaded our light packs and rifles from the weasel and built a small fire for lunch.

While we ate our light lunch, I saw John walk out

away from the fire about thirty feet; again he stood facing the northwest, standing silent and motionless.

Quietly, I asked Ed what the trouble was. Ed shook his head and muttered, "Beats me. I can't figure it out."

I began to worry about this stalwart mountain man, who obviously had absolutely no fear of man or beast, and I decided to keep my eyes open and watch him.

After lunch we shouldered our packs and rifles and commenced the hard, nearly vertical climb of the massive peaks towering over us. My heart pounded and my lungs ached and burned from my labored breathing and the high altitude. Sweat ran down my face. I noticed that Ed also was sweating and breathing hard from the climb, but John was climbing easily and his breath came normally.

Ed and I were both in good physical condition from hunting trips and frequent wilderness treks, but I marveled at the ease with which John made the ascent. During the afternoon, we made frequent stops to scan the surrounding mountainsides for the elusive Dall sheep and saw several at scattered locations, but none which would legally qualify with the three-quarter curl of the horns.

Having reached a nearly level plateau on the mountainside, we decided to make camp there, since the sun was sinking into the west and our weary bones cried out for rest. We unrolled our sleeping bags and set up our base camp.

I noticed again that John was gazing to the northwest and that he had once more become strangely quiet. John's actions up to this point had appeared to be normal, but now he sat down beside the small alcohol stove on which we were heating water to make tea. He held his head in his hands and stared at the little stove.

I began to worry seriously. I looked at Ed, but he only shrugged his shoulders and continued with the camp chores. The sun had started to slip behind the mountains to the west; I asked John if he wanted tea.

He never answered. He only continued to sit, staring silently at the stove.

Suddenly John leaped to his feet and started to roll his sleeping bag.

Ed looked solemnly at him. "What's the trouble, John?"

John hesitated, then finally answered: "I go home. My wife just died."

A chill ran down my spine. This didn't make sense to me at all. "What makes you think your wife just died?"

John only stared at me a long time. "I know. She just died," he said.

Ed said, "John, why don't you wait until morning, and if you still feel the same way we'll all go out together."

John shook his head. "I go now."

I started to say something to John, but I saw Ed shake his head at me, so I remained silent. Within three minutes, John had his pack made up and, without a word, turned and started down the mountain in the gathering darkness.

I turned toward Ed. "Can he possibly make it down this mountain in the dark?"

"Well, he can see as well at night as we can in the daytime."

I finally crawled into my sleeping bag, but lay awake, pondering the mystery of John's departure. I felt the eerie presence of something I could neither grasp nor understand, so I lay awake for several hours, deeply concerned by what I had seen.

The strange feeling stayed with me through the next morning. I commented on the matter, but Ed said, "I saw something like this once before, but I can't figure it out either."

By noon, both Ed and I had taken trophy Dall sheep, and by sunset we had the meat and the beautiful white hides packed for travel.

The next morning found Ed and me making our way back down the mountain. We found the weasel parked as we had left it. We loaded our packs into the weasel and soon arrived at the pickup and trailer, which were also sitting undisturbed. We loaded the weasel onto the trailer and made our way back to the village. There we stopped to talk to a man sitting in front of one of the old houses.

We asked whether he had seen John and the man told us John had come into the village during the night, borrowed a pickup from a friend of his, and taken off down the road fast.

This all amazed me—that a man could, in the dark of

night, cover the same distance we had previously covered and do it in less than one third the time we had taken. The puzzle deepened in my mind. On reaching the Gulkana airport I told Ed, "I've got to find out more about this. Let's fly up to Delta and find out what actually happened."

Ed shrugged. "Okay, if you want to. You fly, so I can get some sleep."

A few minutes later, I gunned the Cessna engine into full take-off power as we climbed into the sky and headed for Delta. The flight was smooth. I contacted the FAA operator at Delta airport, and turned onto the final approach pattern for a routine landing.

In the airport operations office, I picked up the telephone and called a man I knew and asked if he knew John Little Bear.

He informed me, "Yes, I know John. He came home late last night from a hunting trip. His wife just died night before last. John is at her funeral now."

I asked my friend when John's wife had died. His answer was this: "I don't know the exact time, but it was about sundown."

I swallowed hard and looked at Ed. He shrugged. "Don't look at me. I don't know the answer."

To this day we have never found the answer.

5
Grizzly on the Rampage

The chill of the gray morning crept into the top of my down-filled sleeping bag. I pulled the hood up closer and snuggled deeper into the bag. On the other side of the now cold campfire, my hunting partner, Ed Wardley, snored softly, still asleep. A few hundred yards to the north of us rose the gloomy but high and rugged Denali Mountains, their peaks wrapped in mist and cloud. To the south and east stretched the McLaren River Valley, gray and dismal in the first light of dawn. The wind moaned softly through the mountain pass and down across the wide valley.

I wanted to go back to sleep, but the thought of hot coffee, bacon, and flapjacks drove me out of the warm sleeping bag and I started making breakfast.

Two days earlier, Ed and I had loaded our hunting equipment into my old Dodge Power Wagon and rolled out of Anchorage, our hometown, headed for a two-weeks' vacation of moose hunting in the wild back country of the Denali Range.

We had spent several weeks working on building our own custom .375 Magnum rifles, with hand-carved stocks made for our own measurements and our Seguine skinning knives were honed razor sharp.

We carried staple food supplies and the usual emergency equipment used by experienced Alaskans; we looked forward to two weeks of carefree, easy hunting for moose and caribou.

Our first stop after leaving Anchorage had been at
Paxson Lodge, where we bought lunch and refilled our
long-range gas tank. At Paxson we had talked to other
hunters, who had reported several moose kills along the
Denali road, but the hunters had also complained of the
scarcity of caribou.

Our first day of driving the Denali gravel road took us
back one hundred and thirty miles to the little village of
Cantwell, high in the mountains and not far from the
main gate of Mt. McKinley National Park. All along the
road, we saw several groups of cow moose with yearling
calves, but after carefully scrutinizing each group with
binoculars, we were unable to find any animals with horns
and since shooting a cow moose in this section was illegal,
we continued our slow trip into the mountains.

Our first night of camping out was beside a small
stream just north of the FAA station at Summit. When
we had gone through the routine of setting up our simple
camp by unrolling our ground cloths and sleeping bags,
and building a small cooking fire, we sat and watched the
evening turn into night and saw the stars come out in
countless legions.

In the distance we heard the lonely, haunting howl of a
lobo wolf beginning his night hunt. The childish yapping
of coyotes died out and again we heard the wolf howl,
singing his lonely, ageless anthem of hunting and the wilderness. His voice was a wild, clear tenor that reached
deep inside a listener.

While cooking breakfast on our second morning out,
Ed and I discussed moving into the Chistochina-Nabesna
area of eastern Alaska to continue our hunt and also do
some sightseeing. A passing hunter told us that large
herds of moose and caribou had been seen in the Slana
area, so we decided to move that way.

Late that afternoon we arrived at Chistochina Lodge,
where we stopped for dinner and spent nearly three hours
talking to the operator of the lodge. He told us of sighting some moose that morning, crossing the road near
Slana, so we made camp that night about one-half mile off
the highway.

Just as we unrolled our sleeping bags, I looked up and

saw a young bull moose standing in a clearing uphill about three hundred yards away.

I whispered, "Go ahead, Ed."

He slipped a cartridge into the chamber of his rifle, raised it quickly, and fired. The rolling echoes of the rifle blast bounced among the trees and the young bull dropped in his tracks.

After cleaning and quartering the moose, we hung the meat high in the tree branches to cool, then turned again to our sleeping bags, happy and tired.

Shortly after midnight we were awakened by an uproar of snarling, snapping, roaring, and bawling that sounded like a civil war had erupted on the hillside under the tree where we had hung the moose meat. Ed and I grabbed our rifles and flashlights and leaped to our feet.

In the beam of the flashlights we saw what appeared to be two young grizzlies fighting over some of the moose meat which they had pulled down from the tree. We both fired our rifles into the air and shouted and swore at the bears. One of the grizzlies wheeled and ran, a front quarter of moose meat hanging from his jaws. The other bear stood his ground, with his front paws on part of the moose meat, growling and bawling and snapping his teeth. His eyes glowed like two bright rubies in the beam of our flashlights and I felt a cold chill deep in my stomach.

Ed, veteran Alaskan hunter, whispered, "I don't think he'll charge. Let's fire two shots, then reload darn quick, because it may get crowded around here in a hurry."

I grabbed for my pistol belt with its .44 Magnum Smith and Wesson and snapped two more cartridges in the rifle magazine. We both fired again and the grizzly slowly backed away into the brush, dragging a quarter of moose meat with him.

We stood at full alert for nearly twenty minutes, playing the flashlight beams back and forth across the birch and alders, but all remained still. I felt cold sweat on my neck and in the palms of my hands.

"I don't think they will be back, but we had better stay awake at any rate," Ed said.

We soon had a roaring campfire going and spent the remaining night hours warily drinking coffee, our rifles at the ready. After what seemed years, the eastern sky lightened into dawn and a red sun climbed slowly over the horizon. We broke camp, packed the one remaining quarter of moose meat in the old Dodge, and made our way slowly back to the highway.

While having breakfast at the cafe in Glenallen, we told two other hunters about our experience during the night. One of them remarked, "So that was what all the shooting was about. We were about two miles from you fellows and it sounded like the Battle of the Bulge."

About this time, a state fish and game enforcement officer came into the cafe with a serious look on his face. He asked whether we were hunting in the area. We told him about our night encounter.

"Fellows," he began, "I need help, and I need it bad. About two hours ago, a big Toklat grizzly killed a little Indian girl and badly mauled a woman near the village of Nabesna.

"An air rescue plane is on the way in to pick up the woman, but one of the men wounded the bear with several shots from a .30-30 rifle, and the bear is still loose in the canyon behind the village."

I told the officer this was about eighty miles from where we had been last night, and the officer told me, "This is a different animal entirely. The people up there have been watching this big boy for several days, and I was afraid something like this would happen."

The officer turned to the other two hunters at the lunch counter. "Would you two like to volunteer to help track down this bear?"

One man shook his head. "Better count us out. All we've got is a .30-06 and a .308, and I don't think those would do the job."

Ed stood up quietly and told the officer, "My partner and I both have .375 Magnum rifles, and I know that country well. We'll try to help if you want us to."

The officer and Ed and I got out a map of the area and marked the location in which the fatality had occurred. The officer pointed to a canyon shown on the map.

"Well, why don't you two work this canyon. I'll get some help from Slana or Chistochina, and we'll take the other two canyons to the east of you."

We paid for our orders and went out to the old Dodge. I asked Ed what our chances were.

He sounded grim. "Somebody has got to stop that man-killer before he makes another kill. Once they go after a human, they get bolder and bolder."

I pushed the old Dodge hard and headed down the highway toward the Nabesna cutoff. As we rattled along, I thought about facing what lay ahead and Ed must have read my thoughts. He said, "The old boy may be clear into Canada by now."

I told Ed I thought that most wounded animals tried to hole up somewhere when injured, but Ed replied, "Yes, but that doesn't always apply to a grizzly. He is mighty unpredictable."

This comment didn't ease my mind any.

When we arrived at Nabesna village, the rescue plane was just landing on the dusty gravel strip. I walked over to where the little girl's body lay covered with a blanket and her sad remains brought a feeling of sorrow and anger to my heart. About twenty yards away lay the injured woman on a stretcher. Her face was unrecognizable as a human's, and her teeth showed through a gaping wound in her left cheek.

Two other men, joined by the fish and game officer, bent over the woman and I could see where her left arm had been badly mangled, with fragments of bone pushing through the skin. Bloody remnants of her shredded blouse showed where her left breast had been torn from her shattered and broken body.

Her breath came in bloody, bubbling gasps. The officer and I took a scalpel from the field surgical kit and quickly made an incision in the trachea, with a hold-open and a gauze flap for protection; at once her breathing became slower and easier.

We lifted her body onto the plane stretcher, then into the plane. The officer and the pilot, conferring quietly by the plane, both agreed the woman could not live through the hour, but the pilot indicated he would do all in his power to make it to the Glenallen hospital.

When the plane had lifted off the strip, Ed and I made up light survival packs containing only the barest necessities for "siwash" living in the wilderness. We drove on past the village for about four or five miles, past the old abandoned mines, to the place where the big grizzly had been seen last.

The Indian with us showed us the tracks and droppings of the grizzly and my hair stood on end at the size of the tracks.

Ed whistled softly under his breath. "Boy! This one is really a whopper!"

The Indian climbed back into his old pickup. "This is where I leave you guys."

Ed started up the dry creekbed of the quarter-mile-wide canyon, with me following about ten feet behind.

Ed looked back over his shoulder. "Stay behind me about forty feet, so that if we get charged, one of us will have a chance for a kill."

I took four cartridges from my belt and loaded the big rifle, with a cartridge in the chamber. Each cartridge was loaded with a maximum powder charge and each one of the big blunt Kynoch grain bullets packed over five thousand foot pounds of energy. After I had looked again at the grizzly tracks, the big bullets looked mighty puny to me and I couldn't help wishing they were mortar shells instead.

We pushed on up the canyon and the sun began to sink into the western rim of the canyon. Occasionally, we found spots of blood on the rocks and grass alongside the dry creekbed.

Ed bent down, studying the blood spots, then looked up. "This isn't good. He's gut-shot and must have one hell of a bellyache. He will probably be in a real bad mood if we ever catch up to him."

Several thoughts went through my mind. "What do you think we should do tonight?"

Ed thought a minute. "Only one thing to do—we'll have to take turns keeping watch tonight and keeping the fire going."

All through that long night, we took turns piling wood on the fire and standing alert to every little night sound, rifle at the ready and every sense sharpened to the keenest edge.

At the first light of dawn, we each drank a cup of in-

stant coffee and chewed on a strip of jerky beef. Ed
spoke: "You've got the best eyes and are the youngest.
You take the point today."

We moved on up the canyon, our leg muscles protest-
ing the climb from the previous day, but after pushing
hard for an hour, we began to loosen up and hit an easy
pace. Every two hundred yards or so, I found spots of
blood on the rocks and mossy growth.

Again Ed examined the blood spots. "We had better
look sharp. He's beginning to slow up. Keep your eyes on
the alder clumps and watch for any movement. If he
charges, he's really going to be moving. Be sure to knock
out his front shoulders, then we can finish him off after we
stop his charge."

I gave Ed my 35mm camera, and told him to keep it
ready along with his rifle just in case we had a chance to
get some photos.

He laughed. "We're going to be too busy to take pictures if that old boy shows up."

As the sun rose, the canyon walls around us took on red
and gray hues, and an occasional vein of quartz in the canyon walls sparkled with glittering mica particles, giving an
unreal beauty to the high walls. For a moment the beauty
of the surrounding mountain scenery almost made me forget the deadly purpose of our trip.

Ahead, the rugged canyon began to open gradually into
a mountain pasture with clumps of high grass and the
hated devil's club thorn bushes. Up ahead several yards, I
saw the wide swath of a trail the grizzly had left in the
grass and I heard Ed mutter. "Any time, now."

We moved slowly, step by step, into the pastureland,
the tranquil beauty of it lying all around us.

When we were about halfway across the little pasture, I
caught sight of a flicker of movement in the shade of a
willow clump about two hundred yards ahead. I raised my
hand, and we both froze in our tracks.

I slowly raised my rifle and sighted through the scope.
The huge grizzly lay under the edge of the willows. The
big blond diamond on his back stood out plainly, posi-
tively marking him as a Toklat. I turned my head and
nodded to Ed.

Ed leaned forward and whispered, "The wind is still favorable, so let's try to work a little closer before we shoot."

I nodded and we began our slow, stealthy stalk of the wounded and dangerous beast. When we were about ninety yards from the big bear, the wind suddenly swung around to our backs and almost instantly the grizzly lumbered to his feet; he was standing on his hind legs, bawling and moaning, his long, dish-shaped face swinging back and forth in the wind trying to locate the hated man smell.

I instantly slapped the scope off to the side on its swing mount so the iron sights would be visible, and snapped the safety into the off position. At this same instant, the huge grizzly located us and dropped down on all fours and charged at full speed.

With the sights lined on the brute's left shoulder, I felt the bucking recoil of the big .375, heard the smack, and saw the dust fly as the bullet slammed into the animal's hide. I pumped another bullet into his left shoulder. This shot knocked him off-balance and he staggered sideways, but his forward momentum never slowed.

Once more I felt the bucking roll of the recoil and saw the dust fly from the bear's hide as the powerful Kynoch bullet struck home, this time into the right front shoulder.

The bear rolled sideways in the grass, moaning and bellowing, and his hind legs tore up grass and rocks and bushes as he thrashed wildly. I quickly snapped three cartridges into the magazine of the rifle and pulled a quick bead on his right ear. Again came the booming thunder of the .375 and the bear gave a last, dying lunge toward us, a huge gout of blood gushing from his mouth.

I slammed another shell into the chamber and stood with a bead on the big brute's left ear, but the bear never moved. A low moan bubbled from his mouth as a final breath escaped the massive body. We stood for a good ten minutes, watching for any sign of life.

I felt my knees shake and sweat run down my back.

Ed walked over to me and put his arm around my shoulders. "Good shooting, partner. You hit him just right."

I tried to light a cigarette, but my hands shook and I continued to sweat.

We skinned the carcass of the magnificent animal and found where three .30-30 bullets had lodged in the left forepaw, one just under the hide on the left side and the third just inside the hump between the front shoulders.

The pain and suffering from these puny bullets must have been maddening to the great animal and in his agony he had turned against the humans he thought had caused his pain and suffering. We rolled the large hide, which, we judged, weighed over one hundred pounds, into a bundle and tied it on a packboard.

After a day and a half of working our way down the canyon, we met the state fish and game officer at the site of our first camp and showed him the hide.

"That's him, okay," the man said. He also informed us that the woman who had been mauled by the bear had died within a few minutes after reaching the hospital.

We asked who had shot at this bear with a .30-30, and he told us, "The dead woman's husband.

"I didn't have the heart to tell him to keep his .30-30 for coyotes and rabbits," the officer went on. "The poor fellow is badly broken up at the loss of his family, and he doesn't have a dime to his name."

Ed was, I saw, deep in thought as we hiked out of the canyon with the big bear hide and the fish and game officer.

On arrival at the village, we were met by the dead woman's husband and we gave him the beautiful bearskin. We visited his cabin and found him without sufficient food; Ed suggested we unload all the rations from the old Dodge. We took the canned and dried food into the widower's cabin, then I saw Ed dig down into his billfold and slip some money under one of the cans. The officer and I followed Ed's cue and did the same.

The man had left his cabin for a short while, and we put our coffee cups down and went outside, preparing to leave for home; there we found all seventeen people, the entire population of the village, lined up to shake hands. The smiles and sincere, warmhearted faces made the toil and danger well worthwhile.

On the road home, we rode along in silence for a long

time. Finally Ed came out with this comment: "I didn't want any moose this season, anyway."

I thought for a moment. "I didn't either. Let's try again next season."

6
Veteran Frontier Pilot

During the years I was employed by the Federal Aviation Agency, I spent most of my time traveling around Alaska, visiting the far-flung FAA outposts, flying from one station to another. Thus I made friends with Jack Jefford, a man to whom Alaska owes an eternal debt of thanks. Tall, gray-haired, tanned by Arctic sun and weather, this man has accumulated well over twenty-four thousand hours of flying time in the far reaches of Alaskan mountains and skies, and has spent over thirty-one years flying to serve his fellow man.

He is a legend, and his calm, level gaze and drawling voice belie the hardships and dangers he faced in order to make flying safe for those traveling in and across Alaska. As long as I have know Jack, he has preached safety in flying, and to this cause he has dedicated his life.

One of the first times I flew with Jack Jefford was on a trip to southeastern Alaska. Jack was piloting the Fairchild C-123 and I was riding on a jump seat behind the pilot's position. Also on the flight deck were Lee Burns, the co-pilot, and the air-base commander from Middleton Island. After making a stop at one of the FAA stations, we started a routine takeoff and I listened to the thundering roar of the big Pratt Whitney R-2800 engines in climb power.

The nose of the big plane lifted from the runway and swung out over the North Pacific Ocean, which spread as far as I could see to the east, south, and west. A few moments after takeoff, I heard Jack's voice come over the intercom through my headphones: "Boys, I've got a gear warning light on the nose wheel. Looks like something is wrong."

Jack kept the nose of the plane pointed skyward, gaining all possible altitude, while the co-pilot and flight engineer climbed down into the cargo hold for a look. Jack cycled and recycled the landing gear several times, and the main gear retracted perfectly, but the nose wheel remained locked in a half-retracted position. Lee Burns climbed back to the flight deck and told Jack, "You'd better go have a look."

This time I followed Jack down into the cargo hold and experienced a sinking feeling as I looked at all the cargo stacked on the floor.

Jack studied the situation. He climbed back to the flight deck and radioed the FAA traffic center, notifying them of the problem with the nose wheel. By this time, Jack had turned the big plane back toward Anchorage; I kept listening to the power song of the right engine. I thought I detected a change in its steady beat.

I climbed back to the flight deck and noticed all eyes were on the engine instruments, and that the right engine was beginning to run rough. The cylinder head temperature was climbing a little. Jack changed the power setting slightly.

"I think it will be okay. Let's try to fix that gear problem first."

We went back down into the cargo hold. Jack took another good look. "Fellows, we've got to unload some of the cargo in order to get the plane weight down to a safe level for landing."

We opened the cargo door in the back of the plane and rolled twenty barrels of oil out the door. I watched the barrels as they tumbled slowly end over end toward the Pacific far below. Since each barrel weighed nearly four hundred pounds, we soon had the plane lighter by nearly four tons. Also on the cargo deck were several kitchen stoves for the FAA wives at Yakataga, but since the stoves didn't weigh much Jack decided to keep them on board.

Meanwhile, everyone listening in on our radio frequency had heard all this yakkety-yak about our dumping things into the ocean because of a mechanical problem, and when we arrived back in the vicinity of Anchorage it looked like all the town had come out to the FAA hangar to watch the show.

Jack contacted the hangar and discussed the nose gear problem. The men there came up with several suggestions, such as free fall, but Jack told them we had tried all the tricks in the book.

Jack thought for a moment. "Say! I know something we can try."

Grabbing a fire ax, he began to chop a hole through the bulkhead into the nose wheel compartment. Then he taped a chain onto the end of a broom handle, and, carefully reaching through the hole, looped the chain around the nose wheel strut and pulled the chain back into the hold.

Jack suggested we turn the deck winch around, which we did, but we later found the chain could be tightened securely with a load binder, thus locking the nose wheel into the down position.

Jack flew in a holding pattern for nearly three hours. He finally turned the big plane onto a final approach out over Cook Inlet and lined up with the center line of the runway.

I looked far ahead to the edge of the runway and saw the row of flashing red lights on the fire and rescue equipment lined along the runway, waiting for our touchdown. With a calm, steady hand, Jack brought the crippled plane over the end of the runway and touched down in a very gentle and safe landing. When the plane came to a stop in front of the FAA hangar, Jack turned to us. "Well, boys, we're back home again."

A few years later, I sat across from Jack in his living room while a cheerful fire crackled in his fireplace, and we talked of flights that we had made together. Jack reached far into the past, recalling episodes of flying that have become history on the frontier. He gazed into the fire and spoke slowly.

"Back in 1937, I was flying for Mirow Air Service in Nome, Alaska. At that time, there were only two outfits flying in Nome—Mirow Air Service and Wein Airways, which had its headquarters in Fairbanks. Whenever an emergency arose, it was handled by whichever pilot could reach the scene first.

"I was on a return flight to Nome when I received word there was a very serious illness at Pilgrim Hot Springs that required immediate air evacuation. Pilgrim Hot Springs was an orphanage operated by the Catholic Church west of the Sawtooth Mountains and just east of Imuruk Basin. The hot springs at this location served to heat the buildings as well as help raise the crops.

"There was no regular air service to the orphanage and it got its mail by dog team from Teller. The orphanage was run in a very capable manner by Father Cunningham of the Society of Jesuits. As assistants he had three or four lay brothers who taught carpentry and other trades, and some nuns, who also served as schoolteachers. As I recall, there were probably two to three hundred boys there, most of them of Eskimo descent. They were happy and well cared for.

"The orphanage was tied into the Alaska Communications System network, having contact with the radio station in Nome, and an urgent message from them indicated Brother Hanson, one of the best-loved lay brothers, was critically ill and needed immediate hospitalization.

"I headed on toward Pilgrim Hot Springs, flying a Lockheed Vega, which was a rather hot plane for that part of the country. This plane had a Wasp SC-1 engine, and was a sister ship of the *Winnie Mae*, the plane in which Will Rogers and Wiley Post went down. It was on skis at this time of the year, since the lakes and rivers were frozen and covered with snow.

"I flew over the Sawtooth Mountains, circled the orphanage, and saw a procession start out with Brother Hanson on a sled. I had to land out on the river and taxi in about one quarter of a mile. It was a beautiful day, with the sun shining on the snow, and I saw Father Cunningham leading the procession with his robes flapping. We loaded Brother Hanson into the plane and I didn't pay too much attention to him at that time, since the pilot's and passenger compartments were separate on this plane.

"I took off and flew into Nome to get him to the hospital as soon as possible. This year, we were flying off the sea ice at the edge of Nome and when I landed people from the hospital met me and took Brother Hanson into their care.

"Later that evening, Dr. Markham called me from the hospital. 'Jack, that fellow you brought in from Pilgrim Hot Springs didn't make it. He died just after we got him into town. You might as well take him on back to Pilgrim Hot Springs for burial.'

"The orphanage only had one radio schedule each day, and I knew I could make it back there before time for the next day's radio message, since there wasn't any other way to communicate with them.

"The hospital people brought Brother Hanson's body down to the plane, wrapped in canvas and sewn by hand, and we loaded the body in the plane. I took off and flew back to Pilgrim Hot Springs, thinking about how everyone at the orphanage had loved and respected Brother Hanson. I knew that with the faith the boys had in surgery, they would be expecting Brother Hanson to return to them safe and well. I circled the orphanage again and saw a procession of boys starting out, followed by Father Cunningham.

"I landed and taxied up and saw the group coming toward me, so I shut off the engine and ran as fast as I could toward them, because I didn't want them to see the body in the plane. The boys were running ahead of Father Cunningham, so I stopped them and told them to stand still and wait for Father Cunningham. They said they wanted to see Brother Hanson, but I shook my head. 'No, boys, let's wait here for Father Cunningham.'

"The boys were quite exuberant, but we waited until Father Cunningham came up because I knew he would be in much better shape to deal with this sort of thing than I would. When he arrived, I told him Brother Hanson had died almost as soon as we had gotten him into Nome, so Father Cunningham gathered his little flock around him.

" 'Boys, we have a sad task. Brother Hanson has gone to be in Heaven. You had better go get a sled.'

"The boys took the news stoically, since they were used to seeing death in their homes, on hunting trips, and out on the sea ice. Being not long out of the states, I was used to the way undertakers handled death, with great dignity and polish, and I felt that life on this far frontier was a rough and tough thing. As long as I live, I will never forget the sight of those kids pushing the sled with the body of Brother Hanson, moving slowly across the barren, snowy ground, Father Cunningham walking along behind and his robes flapping in the wind. I knew how keenly they must miss their beloved friend as I started the engine and lifted the Vega off the ice for the return to Nome."

The fire in the fireplace had burned down. Jack got up to put more logs on the fire, then returned to searching his memory.

"I made another flight out of Nome with the Lockheed Vega that I will never forget. After flying all day, I returned to Nome and found everyone all excited. Jack Devine, the territorial senator from Nome, had suffered a severe heart attack, and Dr. Markham from the Nome Hospital said his only prayer for life was to get him to a hospital in Seattle, where doctors had the necessary equipment and personnel to keep him alive. At that time, I was only twenty-seven years old and eager to make a flight to Seattle, and I was probably in better shape than I am now. The Devines had a close friend, Sam Kendrick, who was reindeer unit manager at Nome, and Sam readily volunteered to make the flight to help Mrs. Devine care for Jack on the way.

"We loaded Jack onto a pallet in the plane, with Mrs. Devine and Sam in seats beside him, and we took off for Fairbanks, which was to be our first fuel stop. We left Nome at 9:00 P.M. and, of course, at this time of year it is daylight around the clock.

"After arriving in Fairbanks, I got the plane refueled and we cleared customs and took off for our next stop, which was at Whitehorse, Yukon Territory. By morning, we landed on the airstrip at Whitehorse, which was up on the hill above town.

"When the Canadians found out that we had a very sick passenger on board, they were most courteous and helpful and went out of their way to help speed up our refueling and get us on our way. We soon had the plane ready for the next hop, which was to Prince George, a stretch of 775 miles, and this was darn near the limit of the range of the Vega. At that time, there wasn't so much as a town or a landing strip in between.

"We took off and headed for Prince George, and by this time I was so tired I was a little punchy, but still going strong. I had a bunch of geological maps along, but I found they were not worth a darn and had a lot of vacant and incomplete areas. I checked the compass and picked up a heading for Prince George and began to follow the general course of the Turnip River. I'll never forget that name. About two hundred miles out of Prince George I saw a tremendous black cloud ahead, which was unusual, since thunderstorm buildup doesn't normally occur until afternoon.

"This cloud was far too high to fly over and much too wide to try to go around with the fuel remaining, but the flying conditions weren't too bad, actually, since I had a four- or five-mile visibility and a good ceiling. But it got rough, real rough, with lightning flashing around and thunder booming in all directions, and the roar of hail on those wood wings was terrible. It sounded like the end of the world.

"I was sitting up there in that pilot's compartment, which was separate from the passenger compartment, with a little hatchway opening between the two, and I began to smell gin. Mrs. Devine and Sam figured this was the end of the world and had been passing a bottle of gin back and forth between them to help ease their fears.

"By then we had been flying eight or nine hours and hadn't eaten anything, and they were in a lot worse shape than I was. We finally ran out of the storm and I began to see signs of civilization under us, a house now and then, and at last a set of railroad tracks.

"We were beginning to run low on fuel and I began to search ahead for the town of Prince George. After several more miles of anxious looking, I saw the town and turned for a landing in the little grass cow pasture south of town that served as a landing field. Airplanes were still a novelty to these people at that time, and it looked like the whole town had come out to watch the proceedings.

"It was very hot there in Prince George and the gin had taken its toll on my passengers. I was very apprehensive about their condition and, of course, deeply concerned about Jack Devine, lying on the pallet in the plane, barely breathing. The provincial police officer was a bit put out concerning my two 'healthy' passengers, but I finally started refueling from some cases of gasoline the people had brought out.

"When the refueling had been completed, I fired up and started to take off. Opening the throttle for full power, I saw the provincial policeman come running alongside the plane, signaling for me to stop. I thought Good gosh, we're all going to end up in the pokey. I shut down and taxied back, and the police officer told me that my passenger had his feet sticking out the window.

"Sure enough, I found that Sam had opened a small escape hatch in the side of the plane and, lying down on the seats, he had stuck his feet out the window. I got his feet back inside the plane and closed the hatch, then took off into the sunset, headed for Seattle.

"We got into Seattle about 9:30 P.M., after sixteen hours' flying time from Nome. This was fantastic flying time back then, especially considering the lack of navigational aids and the limited number of airports and places to refuel.

"Poor old Jack, after all the flying we had done, died that night in Seattle. I stayed for the funeral and was one of his pallbearers."

Once again Jack got up and put some logs on the fire, then returned to hunting through his memory, recalling incidents and days of the past.

"I remember an incident that happened some time ago. A fellow named Bud Boding and a passenger were flying up the coast from Seattle in a single-engine Waco that was equipped with floats. Back in those days, planes stopped at Alert Bay and Bella Bella for refueling. There weren't any navigational aids along the coastline then, and all a pilot had to go by was whatever charts he might have in his possession. Nowadays, as you know, all Alaskan planes carry survival gear, and I don't know whether or not the Waco was so equipped, but, anyway, the weather was terrible and getting worse all the time. While flying along this lonely, deserted coastline, Bud and his passenger, a doctor, were forced to make a landing because of the stormy weather and the rough surf badly damaged the plane.

"The plane began to break up in the pounding surf, so Bud and the doctor disconnected one of the floats and, holding onto it, paddled desperately for the shore.

"They managed to fight their way up onto the beach and stood there all alone, soaking wet, with not a dry match between them and no way of letting anyone know where they were. The weather continued to worsen along this western shore of Canada, and their plight began to look more grim with every passing hour.

"They were standing there, just grateful to be alive, when all at once they heard a plane motor and saw a Bellanca come down from out of the overcast and crash into the mountainside high above their heads, killing all persons aboard.

"Fortunately, the Bellanca, owned by Alaska Juneau Gold Mine Company, did not burn. Bud and his passenger made their way up the steep mountainside to the crash site and found that everyone on board had been killed. While searching through the wreckage of the Bellanca, Bud found the survival gear that had been in the plane. So they returned to the beach and made camp.

"With the survival equipment, the situation began to look much brighter for Bud and the doctor, but the high wind and heavy rain made it impossible for any search parties to operate. After several days, the storm abated and the clouds lifted.

"Shortly after that, search planes arrived in the area and found Bud and the doctor on the beach. Because it was impossible for the search planes to land, fishing boats were sent and soon picked them up from the beach. But the irony of the situation was the fact that the search planes had been searching for the Bellanca which had crashed on the mountainside, and, otherwise, never would have had knowledge of the plight of Bud and his passenger."

7
Dawn Requiem Flight

The gleaming silver DC-3 sat silent and ghostlike in the predawn darkness on the parking ramp at Merrill Field in Anchorage. Brilliant night stars glittered in a clear sky, and the cold air carried the faint smell of the tide flats to the west. This was a pungent odor, reminiscent of the salt ocean, the wide expanse of Cook Inlet, of fishing boats and seaport towns. The grim, gray outline of the Chugach Mountains stood like a somber sentinel along the east side of town, waiting patiently for the sunrise of a new day. The town lay sleeping, the night silence lying like a peaceful blanket over houses and vacant streets.

Inside the small operations office next to the parking apron, Walter Gosney, a close friend and long-time bush pilot, leaned against the wall as he talked to the FAA weather teletype operator by phone; the mumbled conversation came to me as he and I made preparations for a special flight over Mt. McKinley.

An elderly bush pilot had died a few days earlier after a long illness and his last will and testament had contained the request that his remains be cremated and the ashes scattered on Mt. McKinley by Walt, who had been his close friend for many years.

Walt had called me the day before to ask whether I would fly as his co-pilot and I had readily agreed, since I welcomed the chance to see Mt. McKinley again and wanted especially an opportunity to take photographs of the massive giant at sunrise.

Seated on a time-worn sofa at the side of the small, brightly lit office were a minister and his assistant. Sitting on the floor between them was a cardboard box that contained the funeral urn which, in turn, held the ashes of the departed old-timer.

An hour earlier, I had replaced empty oxygen tanks with full ones and had inspected the face masks and hoses, as well as the emergency equipment which is mandatory on every plane operating in Alaska.

After the sleepy gas truck driver had departed, I climbed onto the wings with a flashlight and checked the gas tanks and caps, and then checked the oil supply for the two new Pratt-Whitney engines. The two front seats on the left side of the passenger compartment had been removed, giving easier access to the small service hatch which opened over the leading edge of the left wing.

After removing the gust locks from the wing and tail surfaces, I stood beside the plane looking up at the stars and saw the first blush of dawn above the jagged mountain range to the east. Clean cold air and a clear sky promised a good day for flying. The big silver bird sitting beside me seemed to invite me to soar to high places. I loved the old DC-3 and its steady, reliable nature, its willingness to fly whenever and wherever asked.

Walt came out of the office with the two ministers, the older one cradling the cardboard box with its precious contents in his arms, and the four of us climbed into the plane and shut the door. When the two ministers had been belted into the two front seats nearest the hatch, Walt and I climbed into our seats in the cockpit, and I started reading off the preflight check list, while Walt answered each item in his easy, drawling voice.

The starters began to whine and growl, and soon the two engines were rumbling, idling with the deep-throated, satisfying rumble that comes only from radial aircraft engines. I called Merrill Tower on the radio and the voice of the controller came through the earphones, crisp and confident, giving us taxi and takeoff instructions.

As the DC-3 swung onto the center line of the runway, I looked far to the west and saw the snow-capped peaks of the Alaska Range, just beginning to turn from deep rose to the bright pink of first sunrise. Walt's hands moved steadily forward on the throttles and the low rumble of the engines gave way to the crescendo howl of full take-off power. I watched the instrument panel closely, calling off the air speed as the DC-3 sped down the blacktop runway.

The slight vibration of spinning wheels against pavement quickly ended and the lift of the big wings as the plane broke its bonds with earth could be felt. Walt called, "Gear up." I shoved the landing gear handle into the up position and heard the responding whine of hydraulic pumps as the wheels retracted.

The instrument-panel lights blinked "up and locked." We continued our climb out over Cook Inlet, across Mt. Susitna to the northwest of Anchorage, the mountain commonly known as the "Sleeping Lady," since its profile closely resembles a person sleeping with a white mantle covering it. We swung to a northerly heading and continued our climb, with our destination about an hour's flight, straight ahead.

As the altimeter on the instrument panel continued its steady climb, I gazed into the far distance and saw row upon row of high, snow-covered mountains in all directions—ramparts of white with sharp, jagged spires lifting into the blue, shadowed canyons falling away between buttresses of frozen granite, and dark patches of cloud shadow drifting in the dawn sunshine across vertical rock walls. I thrilled at the grandeur of the awe-inspiring scene.

Directly ahead, looming larger as the moments passed, stood the patriarch of North American mountains, the giant fortress of "Mighty Mac," and its companion to the west, Mt. Foraker. Since it stood head and shoulders above the surrounding mountain ranges, I could understand why the Indians and Eskimos called it "Denali," or father of mountains. Its great shadow-covered lesser mountain peaks to the west and all the wilderness of rocky peaks below seemed to pay homage to the silent giant.

Our altitude neared ten thousand feet. I crawled out of my seat and went back to the passenger compartment, where I helped the two clergymen put on the clear plastic oxygen masks and plugged the hoses into the outlets near their seats. I asked the elder of the two ministers how he wanted to conduct the services. Then I explained how we would open the hatch, and how to hold the urn; he agreed that all seemed satisfactory.

Returning to the co-pilot's seat, I told Walt the plans for the services were all in order. He nodded. "Okay, fine. I think we had better get on oxygen now ourselves."

We plugged in our masks and the oxygen had the familiar, dry, slightly stale smell, but my head felt clearer. The throb of power from the two engines continued as the plane climbed steadily and the mighty mountain drew nearer.

The sun had risen full into the heavens by now; the surrounding peaks and spires were lit with the blinding glare of clear sunshine reflected from massive ice fields and glaciers far below. The contrast of the pure white mountains and the cobalt dome of the sky was startling.

Walt made minor changes in the power settings of the engines, which by now were laboring in the high thin air, still clawing upward, struggling for altitude. I looked back into the passenger compartment and the younger of the two clergymen gave me the circled thumb and forefinger sign, signifying that all was well.

When we leveled off near the summit of Mt. McKinley, I took several pictures of the great mountain as we circled the peak at a safe distance. We continued negotiating the slow, gradual circle. I asked Walt whether he wanted to go back and assist with the services.

He continued to look straight ahead for a moment, then shook his head. "No."

I climbed from my seat and went to the rear of the plane, then took a cargo strap from the storage compartment and returned to the front seats where the ministers were sitting. I nodded to the older minister and he knelt in front of the hatch on the left side of the compartment. I tied the cargo strap around his waist and snapped the end of the strap into a D ring in the center of the floor of the plane.

The minister turned to his assistant, who slipped the urn from its box; the first minister placed the urn between his knees, then reached into his parka and removed a service book.

Opening the book, he read the funeral service. I could see his lips move behind the oxygen mask. I looked down at the book and saw part of the ritual, taken from the Twenty-Third Psalm: " Yea, though I walk through the valley of the shadow of death, I will fear no evil, for Thou art with me. . . ."

The minister bowed his head in prayer, then read again. "Into Thy hands, Almighty God, we commend his spirit and his ashes shall return unto the earth from whence they came."

He then looked up at me and nodded, slipping the service book back into his parka, and pulling on his gloves. I swung the locking lever open and pulled the hatch inward and we were hit instantly by a blast of icy air and roaring engine just outside the open hatch.

The minister carefully tilted the urn into the open hatchway, then with a quick twist he opened the urn. There was an instantaneous puff of gray-white ashes into the slipstream, then the urn was closed and pulled back inside the hatch. The minister again bowed his head in prayer, and then he raised his head and stood. I removed the safety strap from around his waist and returned it to the storage compartment.

Returning to the cockpit, I leaned over Walt's shoulder. "His ashes are on the mountains."

Walt never spoke, but only nodded his head, his eyes fixed on the distant horizon. After a few moments, he turned his head and looked back toward the peak of the mighty mountain for a moment, then, facing forward, slowly rocked the wings of the DC-3 three times, an airman's farewell to an old friend. The nose of the plane turned slowly southward toward Anchorage and home; the great mass of the McKinley Range slipped underneath our wings.

We continued our southward journey, the steady drone of the engines the only sound in our ears. I watched the altimeter slowly start to unwind as we began our gradual descent.

With the plane's return to the ten thousand-foot level, I once more crawled out of my seat and went back to the two passengers. After telling them we were again low enough not to need oxygen, I stayed with them while they gratefully slipped out of the masks and unplugged the hoses. I returned to the co-pilot's seat and, after a routine check of the instrument panel and fuel gauges, resumed my study of the beautiful mountain peaks that ranged in every direction as far as I could see.

Gazing to the westward over the rugged Alaska Range, I suddenly spotted a thin vertical column of smoke reaching high into the atmosphere, and I picked up the binoculars which hung behind my seat. I studied the rising column before speaking to Walt.

"It looks like it may be coming from the area of Mt. Spurr."

Walt took the glasses and looked for a while at the smoke column, then agreed. "Go ask the preachers if they want to fly over toward Mt. Spurr for a look-see."

I motioned to the passenger compartment and the younger minister came forward into the cockpit. I pointed out the smoke column, and he immediately asked for the chance to fly over the scene. We banked slowly toward Merrill Pass and Mt. Spurr, which is one of the active volcanoes in Alaska. The closer we drew to the area, the more obvious it became that the crater on the side of Mt. Spurr was the source of the smoke column.

I called Anchorage air route traffic control center on the radio and reported we were flying in for a look at Mt. Spurr. The controller told us he had two other pilot reports of the smoke column, and would we please advise conditions on arrival?

Not many years past, Mt. Spurr had erupted and covered Anchorage with a thick blanket of gray ash, and all regular Alaskan pilots had formed a habit of keeping an eye on the mountain.

As we neared the pass, the smoke column assumed immense proportions and from our altitude it appeared to be nearly five hundred feet wide at the base and reaching well over thirty thousand feet in height. We approached to within ten miles of the crater. I felt the plane shudder from the turbulence and heat and saw the tremendous clouds of gray smoke boiling out of the crater on the side of the mountain.

The sky darkened and the plane bucked and bounced. I told Walt: "Try to hold her steady, so I can get a few shots with the camera."

"Make it quick. We don't want to get much closer."

I pointed the camera through the windshield and took four or five fast pictures, then we banked for a circle and another look at the cauldron of seething smoke and hell under our wingtip. I saw large, house-sized boulders rolling and bouncing down the mountainside as the tremendous pillar of boiling smoke continued to climb into the sky.

I called Anchorage center and told its controller of the estimated size of the base of the smoke column and the large boulders spewing from the crater. After four or five circles and more photos of the eruption, Walt said, "Let's get out of here."

By this time the turbulence had increased and the plane required both of us to man the controls. We turned on an easterly heading toward Anchorage. Clearing the zone of severe turbulence, I once more called Anchorage and told them of the encounter with severe turbulence. The controller stated that he would issue a warning to all aircraft in the vicinity about the conditions.

We flew toward Anchorage. I looked to the east across the wide expanse of Cook Inlet and thought of the old-timer whose ashes were lying high on the frozen ramparts of Mt. McKinley. Then I thought of the thundering eruption of the volcano behind us, and I felt that maybe Mt. Spurr had rendered a fitting farewell salute to the old pilot who had spent most of his lifetime flying among the mountains he loved.

8
Beside Still Waters

How many hours does a man spend in a lifetime dreaming about things that might have been? Or wondering what life would have been like if things had gone differently? How often does the spirit turn inward with sadness or bitterness about things in life we feel we have missed —or things that we have wanted but never attained? Many times I, for instance, have thought that if only things had been luckier for me, or different, I might be farther ahead than I am now.

I remember once when I walked the streets of a large western city, watching the crowd of people around me as they hurried about their business. I had only eight dollars in my pocket, the last remains of self-support. My spirits were at a low ebb and I wondered what I had done wrong.

Why was I at the bottom of the barrel, when once I had known a full degree of success and happiness, with material possessions that left little to be desired?

I watched the shadows lengthening between tall buildings and neon signs and streetlights coming on, one by one. At the corner of a busy intersection I saw a poor, sodden drunk slumped against one of the buildings, tears streaming down his face.

His filthy clothes and a reek of vomit and stale wine hung on him, indicating this was his way of life. I stopped in my tracks and looked at him in amazement. A smell of stale wine or filthy clothes did not cause my amazement, because years of police work had hardened me against the cruelties of life.

Rather, my surprise came from the sudden question in my mind: Why should a man let himself fall to such depths of despair and loneliness? What kind of life had he known before he reached skid row and total abjection? What had caused his total loss of ambition and what had made him give up inwardly?

These questions were in my mind as I stopped beside him and placed my hand on his arm. He turned his bleary face toward me, and his watery eyes tried hard to focus on my face. His thick-tongued speech was nearly unintelligible, but I soon understood that he wanted some money for another bottle of wine.

Past experience told me that more wine would prolong the state of semi-anesthesia, and when it wore off the damage to his physical and mental being would have worsened. A feeling of wanting to help him stole over me and I thought for a fleeting moment of my own limited means. But I quickly put this thought out of my mind, for it was dwarfed by a feeling of brotherhood toward the kind of world this poor, miserable human lived in.

The steady on-off flashing of a neon sign a block ahead caught my eye and I read the letters "Lighthouse Mission." A sudden inspiration gripped me and I felt that here lay my answer.

Slowly, I guided the drunk, stumbling step by step, up the sidewalk toward the mission sign. Reaching the front door, I pushed the knob and opened the door into a foyer with a desk and two chairs. I guided my friend to one of the chairs and a man in a wrinkled suit and tie came through a door at the back of the room and looked at both of us.

I explained that the man beside me was drunk and needed some coffee and something to eat. On a spur-of-the-moment decision, I reached into my billfold and pulled out two one-dollar bills and held them out to the kind man of the mission. I told him I wanted to make an offering for the mission, but this was all I could spare. The gentle-faced man accepted the donation and placed the money in a small box locked in the desk in the office.

I helped him lead my new-found friend down a short

hall to a kitchen and dining hall, where the smell of hot soup and coffee was strong. We placed my friend on one of the benches at a table and his head immediately fell forward on his arms. After trying several times to get some soup and coffee into him, we gave up, and I helped the minister carry him down the hall and into a bunk-room, where we placed him in bed. The minister offered to join me in a cup of coffee and a bowl of savory beef stew, which I accepted.

He bowed his head and asked the Lord's blessing. Then we ate slowly, seated at the end of a table in the other-wise deserted dining room. After several minutes of silence, my curiosity overcame me.

"How many fellows in his condition do you see every day?"

The minister stared at me a few seconds, then shook his head. "I don't know. I lose count."

I then asked whether he had ever found any reason why people hit skid row, and he thought again. "I guess it's a combination of two or three things. I would call it a lack of faith in themselves and the Lord, and most of them don't have the moral fiber to break the hold that booze has over them."

Then he turned to me and asked, "What are you doing down in this part of town, anyway?"

It was my turn to think. I told him I was just looking around and wanted to see the sights.

The minister made a comment that stuck in my mind, which probably had something to do with striking and kindling in me a new will and determination to make something of myself, to launch myself upward.

"You obviously don't belong in this part of the city, and you are young, in good health, and willing to help your fellow man. I would say the sky is the limit for you."

Many times, in the following years, I have had reason to recall the statement the mission minister made that night. I will never forget his parting words to me: "May the Lord bless you and use you to help your fellow man."

A few years later, I stood alone beside a lake deep in the heart of the Alaskan wilderness and watched the sun set in quiet splendor, as the haunting, quavering cry of a loon floated through the shadows along the shore of the lake. Behind me stood my small camp—a surplus army tent, a frying pan, a coffeepot, and a rifle. On the previous day I had started my hike back to the lake to spend a few days alone in meditation. Now I began to take stock of myself. I had just gotten launched on a new job and a career that held a world of promise; I actually didn't have a worry in the world.

But, being a loner, or bachelor, I had been feeling sorry for myself and now realized that I was wasting my time.

A gentle ripple moved along the edge of the lake near the spot where I stood. A soft, nearly inaudible clucking sound occurred near me. I froze, watching the ripples, and out of the weeds and grasses came a mallard hen, paddling slowly through the water. Behind her came a small brood of six or seven small ducklings, paddling frantically, trying to keep up with their mother.

Ducklings . . . like little children. Damn. There it came again—that threat of depression. I wondered how the children looked now. Looking at the situation face to face, I scolded myself: okay, old buddy. If those poor little ducklings can learn to survive in this world—when their only defense will be the power of flight—you had better get on with living yourself. You should be out here on the frontier doing something constructive, like trying to help someone who needs your friendship and encouragement.

My mind flipped back to the man at the mission and his words of counsel came in loud and clear to me now: "Help your fellow man."

I was all right now. I had decided a good course in life would be to try to make friends whenever possible and to be of assistance to a brother human whenever I could.

That night I watched the full moon rise again on its endless trajectory across the heavens, and the brilliant moonlight and the yellow birch leaves near the lake told me this was the waning of another season, sunset days of a summertime past, and the last hours before a big winter freeze-up.

How symbolic this was of human life. Spring, in all its budding glory, to me represented the birth and younger days and years of our life on earth, a time of learning, growing, and gaining strength for the summer ahead.

Summer, with long days of sunlight and fullness of

bloom, was the prime of life—the working, productive years of a human. Summer is the one chance for a mortal on this earth to prove himself and to labor in a good work of service to his fellow men.

Autumn, the most colorful period in nature, shows the advancing years of human life and with it the nostalgia and memories of the past which cannot be relived.

I had to wonder what the sum of my memories would be when the sunset and autumn of life should come to me. I already felt as though I had lived a full lifetime and had known the sweet pleasures of youth, combined with almost overflowing sorrow and heartache. In introspection right now, I found myself standing at the early part of my summertime; I resolved to readjust my sense of values to a level which would bring some degree of satisfaction in my autumn.

By the time my campfire had burned low, I felt at peace with myself and knew I had had the chance, which I had taken, to chart a course for my life. The wandering, swinging compass needle of my spirit had steadied on a new heading.

Again came the quavering musical cry of the loon and this time I felt a new joy, a sense of challenge and usefulness.

I was all right now.

A few weeks later I drove up the highway toward Fairbanks and stopped along the way to have lunch and refill the gas tank. At the lodge I looked at the towering mountain peaks overhead and saw the first coat of new snow, a sure sign that autumn was nearly past and winter just around the corner. In front of the lodge sat an aged Athabascan Indian, his hair as white as the new snow on the peaks. His parka and mukluks bore the traditional emblems of a tribal chieftain or patriarch.

I spoke to him and he answered with a toothless smile and friendly hello. He asked where I was headed, and when I told him I was going to Fairbanks he asked if he could ride along. I returned his smile.

"Sure! Hop in. I'd be happy to have someone to talk to."

As he walked around my pickup, I noticed his back was bent with age and his legs bowed from many years of running a trapline in the bitter cold of winter, as well as from the dietary deficiency common to his people.

Conversation was easy as we drove on up the highway. I told him of my relatively short time in the northland and how I had come to love Alaska. He in turn told me of his life in the Copper Valley and how, as a child, he had witnessed several battles between Indian tribes. He also recalled seeing his first white man when a fur trader came through the valley.

When I asked his age, he told me, "I don't know. About 109, I guess."

He related old legends handed down from his father, incidents that dealt with the Russian exploration of Alaska, and the cruelty of explorers toward Indians. He told of having personally witnessed the big influx of white men into the north during the Klondike Gold Rush and he chuckled when he told of how many Indians knew where there were large deposits of gold but refused to pass the information on to the prospectors.

When I inquired how many children he had, he said, "Oh, lots of them. But I've got over forty grandchildren, and all of them have children by now."

The old chieftain told about bitterly cold days and nights of trying to survive and work trap lines and how, after an exploration party had visited the village, a diphtheria epidemic had decimated the populace.

As we rolled along the highway I heard stories of hardship and terror that made my blood run cold. But I also heard of the good times of his people, and the great love the parents had for their children. The old man told about the great potlatch celebrations lasting for over a week which marked a special occasion or a highly successful hunting expedition. I admired his optimistic outlook on life, and his dry sense of humor kept me in high spirits.

When we were nearing Fairbanks, he asked whether I had a squaw. I shook my head.

"No."

He stared at me in shocked amazement, then laughed and slapped his knee. "You plenty smart guy."

I told him I had been married once, but was single now.

He gave me a big toothless grin and spoke good-naturedly. "Huh, well, I guess you find another some-time."

"Maybe." I was smiling myself. I didn't tell him, but I was pretty sure I would be married before long.

When we rolled into Fairbanks, he invited me to come visit with his sister, so we drove to a log cabin on the edge of town and pulled into the yard. A gray-haired Indian woman, also bent with many years' toil, met us at the door and welcomed us. Inside the cabin an old-fashioned coffeepot sat on top of a cast iron wood-burning stove, and colorful blankets hung on a wall and lay on the bed in the corner.

A man I judged to be about seventy years old rose from his chair by the stove and shook hands. The elderly lady introduced him as her "middle son." Strong coffee and friendly conversation soon became the order of the day.

When I prepared to leave, and said my good-byes, the old chieftain followed me out to my pickup and thanked me for the ride. We shook hands and he told me, "My son, too many young people live much too fast. Take time to talk to your spirit each day."

As we parted, he handed me another bit of sage advice: "When you get another squaw, be good to her and she work a lot harder."

I've thought many times about that day and wished I could have spent several months with that wise old patri-arch of the wilderness. He could have taught me much.

I've reflected about his comment on living too fast, and applied his principle in my own life. I have received an education from the wilderness that has brought me inner strength and made the rugged path of life much easier. In the wild ramparts of mountain and forest I have watched the wilderness creatures at work and at play and have found that they devote a part of each day to work and part to play. Nature has taught them to live with their en-vironment; the sixth sense they use in their everyday fight for survival is both fascinating and surprising to a human.

The beady-eyed little parka squirrel, with his playful yet serious outlook on life, spends the first moments of a new day peering from his burrow, taking stock of the world around him. He looks first to make sure his territory is free of danger and trespassers, then he begins his search for food.

After a breakfast of seeds or tender plants, he is then prone to engage in the carefree social activities of his colony. He will play tag, wrestle with other parka squirrels, and engage in wild foot races, darting in and out under plants and bushes and charging headlong through clumps of grass and low-bush cranberries.

During the harvest time of late summer, his social activities change and he concentrates more on the serious matters of his little world. He starts looking for a mate and works frantically at storing his winter supply of food in underground caverns. On bright, warm, autumn afternoons, his cheerful two-note whistle carries clearly on the air and the warning whistle of a guard squirrel causes an entire colony to vanish instantly.

The Arctic wolf, frequently misunderstood by those who do not know him, shows a degree of intelligence that should be the envy of every human. Several times I have spent a whole day watching a female wolf teach her pups the fine art of staying alive under diverse conditions. Many men, in their fear of the unknown, have related childhood ogre-tales and made the wolf into a deadly demon. Actually, the wolf, in his curiosity, may at rare times spy on man or follow at a respectable distance while a trapper makes his rounds, but the wolf has a healthy fear for and dislike of humans. Unless driven by hunger or rabies, the wolf shuns man entirely.

In his search for food, the wolf may do what comes naturally and dine on game he finds caught in a trap; thus he incurs the wrath and half-truth tales of the trapper. A female wolf and her dog-wolf companion are usually monogamous and spend most of their time working hard at teaching their pups how to find food. Their family life is filled with care for their offspring.

A pack of hunting wolves will follow a large herd of migrating caribou, trailing along behind and pulling down the weaker or sick animals, and thus, according to the laws of nature, help guarantee survival of the fittest.

Beside these still waters and among these rugged mountains I have found the secrets of this strong, beautiful land, and many times I have thanked the Almighty

Creator for showing me a few of the samples of His handiwork. This is my land, my Alaska, and here, by the grace of God, I want to spend my years and here I want to die.

To those who would misuse this land, I say that Alaska is no place for you. Get out while the getting is good. To those who love the beauty and peace of the wilderness I say take your time and move slowly. Look around you, and discover the rare beauties and mysteries that lie hidden at your feet.

Take time to listen for the still, small voice of this wilderness, and your reward will be great. You can never change the wilderness, only destroy it. But the wilderness can change you—and all for the good. It can teach you to live with yourself and it will give you the strength to live with your fellow man. It will build your soul and your body, if you will only look and listen, and heed what you learn.

9
Wilderness Mercy Flight

The weather sequence teletype kept up its incessant clatter in the Federal Aviation Agency Flight Station at Nome, Alaska, while outside on the parking apron a ground crewman made last-minute checks on N-5, the FAA DC-3 with its bright orange tail and wing tips.

A pale, afternoon winter sun cast long shadows across the snow-covered ground, and the soft moan of the wind coming in from the frozen Bering Sea put a biting edge on the sub-zero cold. Dry, powdery snow lifted in small clouds which skidded across the runways and faded into the east, scattering over the tundra and the treeless, rolling hills. To the northeast, the Bendeleben Mountains stood stark and white against a dark blue sky.

Inside the flight service station, I leaned against the counter and watched as Don Hood, a veteran FAA pilot, studied weather reports and filled out weight and balance sheets and a flight plan. The operator on duty kept up a running weather briefing with Don and his co-pilot, commenting on weather conditions between McGrath and Anchorage, our home base and final destination.

As an inspector for the FAA, I had just completed two weeks' routine inspections along the Bering Sea and was eagerly looking forward to being at home. Tomorrow would be my wife's birthday, and I estimated I'd make it home just in time.

I asked Don, "Is there any chance we can make it

home before the stores close? I've got to get a birthday present for my wife." (I had recently remarried.)

Don turned, a smile on his face. "Last-minute shopper, huh? If the weather doesn't get too bad we should hit it about on time."

Don then turned to his co-pilot. "If you fellows are ready, let's get rolling."

The three of us walked out on the apron and pulled our parka hoods up against the knife-edged wind. I followed Don as he performed his walk-around inspection of the plane and removed the gust locks from the control surfaces. He looked up at the sky, then up and down the runways and taxiway. We climbed into the empty DC-3 and I helped Don pull the door shut with a solid thump of the locking handle. Don and the co-pilot climbed into their seats and I swung down the jump seat behind the pilot's position and pulled the seat belt tight across my lap, then snapped the shoulder harness into place. The co-pilot started reading the preflight check list and I listened intently to the chanted litany between pilot and co-pilot.

I admired Don as his hands flicked over the many switches and controls. His quick, confident voice held a calm note which could only be the result of countless hours of flying and familiarity with the intimate relationship of plane and sky.

"Start engines!"

The Pratt-Whitney engine on the right wing growled slowly in protest against the starter and the propeller blades began their slow swing. The sudden cough in the right engine was followed quickly by a similar rumble from the left engine. We sat with the brakes locked while the engines warmed up and the check list continued, and I watched Don as his eyes roamed across the instrument panel.

I clamped the extra set of earphones on my head just in time to hear the controller giving us taxi and takeoff instructions. After a short taxi and the engine run-up, Don swung the DC-3 onto the center line of the runway, then the soft rumble of the idling engines gave way to the full-throated roar of full takeoff power. The co-pilot called out, "V-1," as the plane lifted off the runway and began its climb. I watched the radio compass needle as it swung in

response to the southbound leg of the radio range as Don
set up a course and heading for Unalakleet and our first
position report.

Looking to the northeast, I could barely see the tip of
Mt. McKinley, glowing pink in the early winter sunset,
and my thoughts drifted back to hunting and fishing trips
I had made during my past years in Alaska. I had come to
love this great land and its warm-hearted people intensely.
I recalled glowing campfires beside mountain streams, the
valiant battle of a rainbow trout on a fly rod, and the
coughing grunt of a bull moose beside a small lake.

The drone of the engines relaxed me and I recalled the
many happy hours I had spent flying alone in the sky,
with nothing but the roar of an engine and ramparts of
clouds for company. Now I felt the plane bank gently as
we passed over Unalakleet; I heard Don's voice giving our
position report to the FAA controller as we set up course
and heading for McGrath, near the halfway point on our
trip home. The sky had grown dark and brilliant stars
floated past broken patches of cloud. The DC-3 bumped
and swayed gently as we began to pick up turbulence; I
continued some daydreaming, unaware of what the next
two hours held for us.

The urgent crackle of a voice in the headphones
brought me suddenly upright in my seat.

"November five, November five, this is McGrath radio.
We have a medical emergency. What is your present location?"

Don thumbed the transmitter button and answered in a
calm voice: "McGrath radio, this is FAA November five.
We are estimating twenty minutes west of your station.
Say again the nature of your emergency."

The McGrath controller answered quickly, "The FAA
station at Lake Minchumina has a woman who has critical
childbirth complications and needs immediate air evacuation to Anchorage. Can you assist?"

Don answered, "Affirmative. Please cancel my flight
plan and refile for Lake Minchumina, Victor Airways via
Farewell and Skwentna to Anchorage. What are the
weather conditions at Lake Minchumina?"

McGrath replied, "They are still above minimums and

the runway has been cleared, but the weather is deteriorating."

"We're on our way."

Turning, Don spoke quickly to the co-pilot. "Let's get moving. Sounds urgent to me."

The drone of the engines picked up as the power settings were increased, and the plane banked sharply. The radio compass needle swung to a new heading as we searched for the Minchumina radio range leg. Don's hand flipped the radio switches and he transmitted: "Minchumina radio, this is November five. Do you read me?"

A new voice came in the earphones. "November five, you are loud and clear. We have some blowing snow but are still above minimums. The medical situation is extremely urgent. What is your ETA?"

Don glanced at the clock on the instrument panel, then at the air chart. "We estimate fifteen minutes. Do you have your runway lights on?"

Minchumina answered, "Negative, November five. We have an electrical failure in the runway light system and they are not operating."

Don hesitated a brief second. "Minchumina radio, put a truck at each end of the runway with bright headlights and we'll try to make it that way."

The air in the cockpit of N-5 took on a new sense of urgency, and a trickle of sweat ran down my side. I watched the sweep second hand of the clock move with agonizing slowness, and groaned inwardly, knowing all too well what was ahead. The altimeter began to unwind slowly as we started to lose altitude, and the engines continued their steady beat of power.

Don's hands reached for the throttles as the minutes and seconds continued to march by. Suddenly the radio compass needle jerked quickly and pointed behind us. Don immediately pulled back on the throttles and propeller pitch controls and called out to the co-pilot, "Landing check list!"

Again came the chant as Don and the co-pilot set up for landing. The plane banked sharply as our eyes searched through the darkness, looking for truck headlights at each end of an unlit runway.

"There they are!" I shouted, as I saw the headlights

through the blowing snow. Don turned on the plane landing lights and two blinding beams of light stabbed into the darkness. Under Don's steady hand, N-5 settled smoothly onto the snow-packed runway.

Don turned to me. "Get back there and get them loaded. I'll kill the left engine."

I unbuckled the belts and scrambled for the rear door as the plane rumbled to a stop. I swung the door open and a blast of snow and cold wind hit me full in the face. Already the panel truck was backing up to the door and a man and a woman helped me as we lifted the stretcher into the plane, then strapped it down securely between folded seats.

The man and woman took seats alongside the stretcher and I looked at the face of the sick Eskimo woman. Her face was wet with sweat and twisted with pain. I was glad to hear the roar of the left engine as it came back to life. The woman seated beside the stretcher whispered, "Please hurry. She's already in hard labor and it isn't going right."

I double-checked the door lock lever, then went back into the cockpit and strapped into the jump seat. I leaned toward Don. "Give it all you can, Don. She hasn't got long."

He glanced at me for one second and nodded briefly. Once again the rumble of the engines rapidly built into a crescendo as N-5, running light, leaped down the runway. I kept my eyes on the altimeter as we clawed our way up through the dark, snowy night until we found a level with light turbulence and leveled off gradually, running hard for home.

There were mountains ahead which we must climb. I crawled out of my seat and walked to the rear of the plane. Searching through the emergency equipment, I found a walk-around oxygen bottle with a face mask and returned to the side of the stretcher. Opening the valve, I sniffed the mask for oxygen, then placed it gently but firmly over the agonized face on the stretcher and tied the bottle down alongside with a cargo strap.

A glance at the woman sitting in the seat revealed tears running down her face as she gripped a rosary in her hands. The Eskimo woman on the stretcher seemed to breathe easier. I felt the pulse in her neck; it was strong and steady.

Returning to the cockpit, I told Don, "She's still with us."

The plane banked slowly as we passed over Farewell and started climbing for Rainy Pass, a mere notch in the Alaska Range of mountains ahead of us. The radio compass needle steadied on the Skwentna radio range leg, our guide to safety over a solid fortress of rock wall.

A short time later, Don said, "Well, we're through the pass and over Skwentna. Let's head for home!"

Don was on the radio again. "Anchorage center, this is FAA November five. We have a medical emergency aboard, situation critical. Will you please have an ambulance and doctor standing by on the runway?"

The controller's voice boomed into the headphones: "Affirmative, November five, the emergency equipment is on the field. We've been expecting you."

I heaved a sigh of relief, then prayed quietly, "Heavenly Father, if it be Thy will. . . ."

Returning to the passenger compartment, I saw the woman on the stretcher twisting and moaning. I told the man and woman beside her: "We're almost there; an ambulance, and also a doctor, is waiting at the airport." Relief flooded their faces.

Ahead, the glow of lights on the clouds marked the location of Anchorage, but the feeling of urgency still penetrated the cockpit as Don and the co-pilot started the landing check list. Turning on the final approach out across Cook Inlet, we saw the bright glow of the approach lights and, beyond them, twin rows of runway lights. To the left of the runway lights were several flashing red lights, marking the location of the rescue equipment.

From underneath came the whine of hydraulic pumps as our main gear went down, and the lights on the instrument panel blinked "down and locked."

FAA November five floated gently down to the runway so smoothly I couldn't tell when we touched down. As we rolled past the rescue equipment, I looked back and saw the ambulance lead a wild scramble as the rescue squad tried to catch us.

Don braked easily to a stop, and willing hands were

soon reaching for the stretcher. After the ambulance left, we taxied to the apron and the propellers unwound. N-5 stood silent and empty. We walked across to the parking lot and no one spoke. Finally, Don said quietly, "See you guys later."

We were home and I felt tired and drained and gave silent thanks for this cool veteran pilot, to whom saving a life was a routine day's work.

(*Author's note:* Don Hood, a good friend, a gentleman, and one of the finest pilots Alaska has ever known, gave his life in a tragic plane crash on the tide flats of Cook Inlet on October 1, 1970. Don was a friend to all who knew him, and his passing left a void in many hearts. The woman in the story above recovered in good shape. I never knew her name or where she lived. On her arrival at a hospital in Anchorage, she had to undergo an emergency Caesarean section. The baby did not survive.)

10
Earthquake!

A gray overcast Alaskan sky made a symbolically somber lid for a Good Friday morning, I thought as I parked my car on an icy Anchorage street. The temperature was at zero on March 27, 1964, and the foot-thick snow I moved through covered ground frozen rock-hard.

Snow along the edges of the streets was dirty with a late winter collection of grime. I kept wishing the sun would shine to help relieve the post-winter blues. Still, as I headed for my office at the Federal Aviation Agency, my thoughts were mostly dominated by some cases I was working on. Digging into papers on my desk, however, I allowed myself the luxury of remembering that the sun should soon be out. And I had been planning a spring hunting trip into the high glacier country east of Anchorage.

My work went well, and through my mind raced a list of food items and equipment to take on the trip.

More important, this was to be a day for celebration. Life, our finances, and the assurance of the home my wife and I had wanted looked good. Long struggles and hard work on the job had begun to show results.

We were actually in the process of buying our new home. For the present, my wife, a fashion buyer at Caribou's Department Store, and her boys and I occupied a duplex. Our home in the Turnagain area was on a high bluff overlooking Cook Inlet, an arm of the Pacific Ocean lying on the west side of Anchorage. At this time of the year the inlet carried countless tons of jumbled, broken piles of pack ice in and out with the tide. Each movement of the ice caused a grinding noise sometimes audible over the sounds of city traffic. I also remembered that, after work today, I would meet my wife. We had looked forward to this day, for we would be buying the last of the home furnishings we needed.

As I dug into the papers before me now, my phone rang. A fellow worker who had just returned from a road trip in the north end of the valley said he had seen hundreds of moose migrating northward, leaving the valley. Odd, I thought, since at this time of the year moose herds are pasturing in the valley and their migration into the mountains occurs later in the spring.

Later that Good Friday morning I received another phone call, this one from the Talkeetna FAA station, which confirmed the earlier report. Someone else had seen moose and wolves moving rapidly northward. I was worried. An unannounced wildlife move of this size meant something was wrong somewhere. But my work became so demanding I had to give it my full attention.

At five o'clock I drove to meet my wife. Light-hearted, Carol left her store, so we could go to the downtown shopping area and Fifth Avenue. Fifth Avenue in Anchorage on any Friday evening is filled with shoppers, business people, and couples going to restaurants and parties. Happiness filled me as I walked with this tall blonde beauty on my arm. It seemed nothing could go wrong with life now.

Carol soon found the washer and dryer she wanted. We were discussing lamps we needed as we headed for the appliance store's front door at 5:36 P.M. About ten feet from the door I felt the floor start the familiar repetitious shaking of a gentle rolling earthquake. I smiled and thought, Here we go again. Since I'd lived in Alaska there had been several mild earthquakes of varying intensities, but damage had been no more than slight.

After a few seconds, I knew this was much stronger than the usual tremor and by the time we had reached the door the store's hanging lamps were crashing and banging together.

I told Carol to hang onto me. We staggered outside

and I grabbed hold of a parking meter post. The building behind us creaked and groaned and the air was filled with the rapidly growing thunder of buildings around us twisting and complaining, agonized giants in death convulsions. The ground was jerking and rolling under our feet and it took all the strength I had to hold Carol up and grip the parking meter.

Fifth Avenue was heaving and bucking like the waves of a turbulent sea. My wife's head whipped back and forth on her shoulders; I pulled her tight against me. People ran out from bars and stores down the street, and the world around us rolled and twisted. It was impossible for anyone to stand.

People were sprawled in the street and on the sidewalks, trying unsuccessfully to crawl on hands and knees. Carol's face was white and she whimpered like a little girl. My mouth was dry and my stomach felt knotted into a tight ball.

Across the street a pole snapped. When the first high-tension wire hit the street a blue arc flashed out and a rolling boom echoed down the street. A hot wire writhed like a serpent spitting fire, then went limply silent as power failed all across town. From a few blocks to the east came a tremendous shuddering roar with a thick cloud of dust lifting high in the air as the Penney Building collapsed.

Carol gasped.

"What if the ground comes apart!"

Within an instant the ground fifty yards from us split open with a deafening roar. We watched as a chasm about one hundred feet wide and two hundred feet deep opened up with an ear-splitting crack, shaking us with its vibration. Several houses toppled slowly into the yawning gap.

I saw a man stagger, lose his balance, then fall end over end like a rag doll into the crevice. With another rending crack, the chasm closed up, then repeated this ghastly process several times. Each time it opened it gulped down into its open jaws houses and cars falling like helpless toys to a terrible finale.

We were barely able to hold our position at the parking meter. My own strength was nearly gone. I stared horror-stricken and sickened at the rolling ground and the people-devouring hole I could do nothing about.

Amazingly, in the midst of this hell, words from the Twenty-Third Psalm pierced my subconscious: "Yea, though I walk through the valley of the shadow of death, I will fear no evil, for Thou art with me...." I breathed a prayer: "Eternal Father, grant us Thy mercy...."

It was strange that neither thought nor fear of personal death entered my mind. My only concern was to get my wife and the boys out of this wreckage safely.

After a nerve-shattering four and a half minutes, the terrible roar subsided, and the heaving ground began to calm. Somehow we crossed the street to find our car still rocking on its wheels. A silence so deep it was deafening by contrast set in for three or four minutes. Then the screams of the wounded and dying, and the wail of police and ambulance sirens filled the eerie darkness.

Ominous silence filled the inside of our car as we drove. After school hours, the boys would have been alone at home. We headed for the Turnagain area where we lived.

At the foot of a hill we found a main road cut across by a crevice. Tires squealing, I backed up, gunning the car for a rerouting. Soon it was obvious something was wrong. People and cars were hurrying north toward our neighborhood.

Several blacks from home I knew something didn't look right. Where our house had stood in a tall grove of spruce trees I saw only gray skies and the expanse of ice floes in Cook Inlet. This had been a high bluff over the inlet. Now—nothing. Carol buried her head in my shoulder and cried out, "Oh, dear God." My hands hurt from their tight grip on the steering wheel. Sliding to a stop, we saw people milling about on an entirely new cliff.

The boys, who had been standing numbed and ill, moved toward us. We threw our arms around each other and then looked.

Our duplex, broken in two, was perched precariously on the edge of this new chasm; a large crack in the ground ran the length of the block. Over the edge of the cliff the ground was scrambled and broken as though a giant plow had turned furrows for spring planting.

About fifty homes lay at our feet in an ugly mass of

wreckage stretching down about two hundred feet to a new shore line. We stood in numbed shock as a wave cluttered with debris and chunks of ice swept in with ease and stealth, then mockingly slipped back out again. The rising and falling wail of sirens coming from downtown told us city rescue equipment was hurrying in all directions.

I looked at the faces of friends around me and saw eyes glazed with terror; an old man was vomiting, his eyes wet with tears. Hushed people shook their heads, not yet comprehending the loss of loved ones and homes. My mind was reeling and I felt very tired.

My wife and I climbed down into the wreckage of our house, but I kept my eye on the open back door in case it started to shake again. The inside of the house was a total ruin, with a few of our possessions in a scrambled heap but most of our property gone through the gaping floor. The only things we had time to save were a few pieces of clothing, one bed, and a rug. Within a few minutes the ground started to roll again from the aftershocks. I got my wife out of there. A crazy thought ran through my mind as the shocks picked up: their tempo matched Lawrence Welk's "one anna, two anna, three. . . ."

Carol voiced the thought that was on my mind. "We've got to find some safe sleeping place. Let's go over to Mark and Mildred Smith's house and see whether we can stay with them." We found the Smiths, our closest friends, safe, their gracious home relatively undamaged. They welcomed us warmly.

I returned to our neighborhood to try to help. When I left my car, a neighbor told me a woman was trapped inside one of the wrecked houses. With two other men, two flashlights, and a chain saw, I climbed down into the splintered remains of a house, and after prowling through two rooms heard crying coming from under some boards. We pried frantically at loose rubble and located a chest of drawers with a large plank across it.

Under the chest was a young woman whose legs were pinned so that she couldn't move. I pulled fiercely on the saw's starter rope and felt a blaze of anger shoot through me when the saw didn't start immediately. After about twenty-four yanks, the saw roared into life, and I cut the plank, while one man heaved on the chest and the other lifted the woman free.

All night, search parties combed the wrecked houses. Part of the bluff area, including what had been our new home, washed out to sea with the receding seismic wave. Rescue helicopters hummed overhead, their landing lights acting as eyes to search for survivors. The copters picked women and children off debris and ice floes which had been washed out into the inlet.

During the night soldiers and airmen from nearby military bases arrived in the area. Hot soup and coffee from army field kitchens saved the night and the following days for many of us. During the dark early morning hours words from the navy hymn went through my mind: "Eternal Father, strong to save, whose arm can still the restless wave...." I knelt, alone, in the snow and darkness, to thank God for His deliverance. I could not hold back the tears that ran down my face. I knew my family would be all right.

But many persons in our neighborhood did not come through that terrible night. Yet, working with the other survivors, I felt and saw how this nightmare was welding courageous individual spirits into a close unit fired with determination to pull through. During those grim hours these undefeated people taught me a lesson. They helped each other, sharing meager belongings, lending moral courage and support. Many times I heard "We aren't licked yet," and "We'll figure out something."

A new bond of friendship and sense of usefulness was born for me that night.

The next day our family began a difficult existence that included shortages of food and water and cooking what food was available over a cantankerous camp stove. I did what I could to help rehabilitate neighbors, and to restore order where I worked. My wife, whose job had been destroyed along with Caribou's Store, worried about her boys.

We sent them by plane to the home of their grandparents in Oregon. Carol suffered the strain of being without her sons, and the severe hardships of the next few weeks, without complaint. But in the night hours I felt tears on her cheeks. I began to understand that things were never going to be the same again.

Finally, she said she could no longer accept life in Alaska. My heart was breaking, but I agreed to leave. Soon we were on a highway going south toward Oregon. At the border of Canada I stopped beside the road and stepped out of the car to look back toward the country I loved. I thought of the people lost, and of the people I felt I was abandoning; of unpeopled valleys. In my mind I could see my little cabin near the lake surrounded by quiet mountains. I felt the grandeur of riotous sunsets, and pictured the moose standing in groves of birch and aspen.

I knew I owed safety, security, and a way of life of her choice to the woman beside me.

Yet, at that moment, I felt I was alone on earth, and a wave of sadness and depression came over me.

Security for the family came quickly, with my new job. Nevertheless, at night and whenever I was alone, I dreamed of hunting trips in the mountains, of campfire smoke beside a lake at night, and the haunting cry of a loon. Though I tried for the sake of those around me to adjust to this new life, I was increasingly aware of a need to turn north once more. This time, I knew, it would be alone.

The memory of my home in the wilderness had haunted me during the months I lived in Oregon. Then the time came when I was offered a new position in Anchorage. Here was what I had been waiting for! A chance to return home.

A few days later, preparations for the trip north had been completed, and when I crossed the border into Canada, skies were cobalt blue. My spirits rose and soared beyond the Canadian Rockies to the rugged ranges of Alaska.

Since my return several years ago, I have reestablished myself completely, and, with endless hours' work, have built a second weekend log cabin. Many nights as I have camped under the stars I have prayed my own personal prayer of thanksgiving to the Almighty for permitting me to return home to Alaska.

11

Search for Klondike Treasure

An idea stuck in my mind and kept bothering me. For a long time, I had heard stories of the old prospectors and trappers and how they spent months in the wilderness with only their packs and rifles, running traplines and living off the land in apparent ease and good health. I wanted a taste of the freedom they must have known. Since my work with the FAA had required considerable travel in the Alaskan bush, I had voluntarily taken an Arctic survival course and found out from actual experience that a human could live in the Arctic wilderness with some degree of comfort and good health.

Some months earlier, I had made the acquaintance of an old trapper named Charley. Charley had immigrated to Alaska from his native Finland in 1935. With a herd of several thousand reindeer, and accompanied by his father and other men, he had brought the reindeer herd across the Arctic ice cap on foot and had survived months of severe storms and weather. I told Charley that I wanted to spend two or three weeks alone in the mountains, living off the land, and Charley readily endorsed the idea.

While looking at a Geodetic Survey map of the McCarthy area, Charley pointed out an area east of the Kennicott Copper Mines, where he said an old wagon trail ran through the mountains. Supplies had been hauled by mule teams to prospectors during the Klondike gold-rush days.

I studied the map closely and saw where the old Goat

Trail led across the mountains from the headwaters of Dan Creek across Skolai Pass and on to the Yukon Border. I had flown over this section of the Wrangell Mountains and knew they were high and rugged, but the beauty and grandeur of the remote, lofty peaks appealed to me. I wanted to get back into the area and explore the old abandoned way stations, camps, mines, and the long unused trail.

The idea gripped me and the siren call of adventure ran hot and strong in my mind. With my two weeks' annual vacation coming up, I applied for and received an additional week's leave without pay in order to put my plan into effect. I decided to spend at least two weeks alone on the old Goat Trail, living off the land, enjoying the scenery, and exploring the remains of a bygone era.

I called a friend at Glenallen who owned a Super Cub and he agreed to fly me into an old, seldom-used airstrip east of McCarthy, where I could start my trip into a wild part of the country which had seldom seen the footprint of a white man.

One of my friends who heard of my plans said, "You must be nuts. That is right in the heart of grizzly country."

I had already discussed this danger with old Charley, who was very wise in the ways of the wilderness, and after hearing his considered comments and advice, I felt the danger from wildlife was far less than the danger from weather. From what I had learned in survival school, coupled with Charley's advice, I began to gather the equipment needed for the trip.

My lightweight aluminum pack frame held a large waterproof nylon pack; tied under the pack was my down-filled mummy-type sleeping bag with its waterproof bag and ground cloth. In order to keep weight to a minimum, I eliminated all items that were not absolutely necessary.

Survival equipment included wooden matches sealed in paraffin, an engineer's compass, a mapping compass, a small flashlight, a small pair of pliers, a length of fine steel wire for snares, area maps, a rugged, sharp skinning knife and stone, a small steel signal mirror, a fifty-foot roll of nylon cord, and a twelve-by-twelve-foot square of plastic sheeting.

Clothing items were simple: a down-filled jacket, lightweight nylon rain poncho, strong mountain boots with extra laces, wool shirt and wool pants, several extra pairs of heavy wool socks, gloves, light wool sweater, and an extra suit of double-layer long underwear. A knit wool stocking cap and sunglasses slipped into the pocket of the jacket easily.

Studying the seasonal weather reports, I thought of the chances of sudden snow squalls in the high places, but the long-range aviation forecast looked like a strong chance for sunny days and starlit nights. My firearms consisted of a .22 Colt Woodsman pistol in a belt holster, with three extra boxes of ammunition in the pack, and a short-barreled Springfield rifle which had been converted to a .308 Norma Magnum caliber, just in case an argument with a bear became inevitable. The little pistol would provide meat for the cook pot and the remainder of the food items that I carried were highly concentrated and dehydrated.

The food package included dried peaches and apricots, raisins, small blocks of cheese, dried beef jerky, blocks of brown sugar-bran concentrate, several packages of hardtack, beef bouillon cubes, powdered green pea soup packets, and some hard candy.

Tucked away in a side pocket of the pack were a roll of fishing line and a small assortment of fish hooks and dry flies in case a hungry rainbow should be lurking in one of the high mountain lakes.

Checking and rechecking the list of items and equipment, I finally decided, with Charley's approval, that the list was complete. The pack and contents, with sleeping bag attached, weighed in at an even thirty-six pounds. A small, compact pair of binoculars hanging on a neck strap completed the kit.

The warm summer sun beat down as the Super Cub lifted from the runway at Gulkana Airport; to the east Mt. Sanford and Mt. Drum stood in beautiful, clear relief against the morning sky. The little red and white plane climbed steadily and eagerly as I settled back to enjoy the panorama of magnificent scenery which passed slowly under the wingtips.

I looked far to the south and saw the thin blue line of

the Pacific Ocean in the distance, and, to the southeast, the sawtooth spires of the St. Elias Range lifted into the azure sky. More to the east, the ragged outline of the Wrangell Range stood in an endless procession of mountain peaks which marched on across the border into the Yukon Territory of Canada.

Passing over the small village of Chitina, the pilot banked on an easterly heading toward the village of McCarthy, which, in years past, had been known as the railhead for the large Kennicott Copper mines. After providing untold wealth in the form of rich copper ore, the mines were closed down and Mother Nature began her work of hiding the scars of man's toil.

Rust, undergrowth, moss, vines, and a myriad of plants combined to cover the remains of the old railroad bed and the miscellaneous pieces and parts of long-abandoned machinery. A few old, weatherbeaten houses, some still occupied, huddled around what was once the main street of a remote mining village.

The little airplane passed over McCarthy, and the Wrangells, which were to be my home for two weeks, loomed to the left and ahead. Reaching the point where Dan Creek joined the Chitina River, we banked slowly to the northeast and soon the faint outline of the abandoned airstrip near the end of the old Goat Trail came into view.

The pilot turned into the wind and made a low pass over the runway to inspect its condition, and, circling once more, he touched down and rolled to a stop. I had given the pilot a duplicate map of the one I carried, with my route and estimated itinerary penciled in red. We agreed the plane would fly over me every fifth day and we would communicate by the standard hand signals used between aircraft and persons on the ground.

On each map I wrote three extra signals to be used to indicate to the pilot whether I intended to remain on the trail longer than planned, if so how many days longer, and whether or not to contact my home.

The pilot gave me a small two-inch-by-twelve-inch roll of bright yellow plastic strips, each six feet long, to use as ground panels for signaling aircraft. He wished me good luck and said he would notify other pilots at Gulkana Airport of my unusual vacation trip. With a friendly handshake, he closed the door of the plane and gunned the engine for takeoff. Circling above the lonely, deserted airstrip, he rocked the wings of the Super Cub and disappeared in the direction of Chitina.

After the plane disappeared I stretched lazily in the warm summer sunshine, took a drink of water from my canteen, then studied the Geodetic Survey map and took compass bearings on the three major mountain peaks to the north, west, and east to verify my location. Due to the many thousands of square miles of mountain peaks in Alaska, many of the lesser peaks have no name, only an altitude designator, and thousands of these peaks don't even have this recognition. Thus the matter of establishing a person's exact location can be, and frequently is, a matter of life and death.

To the east of the gravel plateau where the airstrip was located, I saw a dense stand of spruce and birch trees and from this direction came the gabble of feeding wild geese. I shouldered my pack, picked up my rifle and loaded it, then swung off toward the sound of the feeding geese.

Working my way around the edge of the grove of trees, I could make out the faint signs of an ancient roadway. I knew I was off on the adventure of a lifetime. As I came around the end of the stand of timber, I saw a small lake which had been hidden from sight. I dropped down lower into the undergrowth and began a stealthy approach to the end of the lake, where I had heard the honking of the geese. Looking closely, I saw nearly three dozen Canadian Honkers floating on the surface of the lake, busily feeding and talking among themselves, enjoying the sunshine and completely unaware of my presence. I dropped down on my stomach and began to Indian-crawl toward the geese, moving gently, a few inches at a time.

With nearly fifteen minutes of easy crawling through the grass, I came within ten feet of the edge of the lake, where I could plainly see the geese feeding. I lay for nearly thirty minutes, watching them feed and admiring their beauty and listening to the music of their soft conversation.

How I admired the old gander who stood guard. His neck was erect and his penetrating gaze roamed the vicinity, alert for the danger of intruders or predators. His head turned from one side to the other so fast my eyes were unable to follow the movement.

The soft, cool mountain wind riffled the calm surface of the lake, and the warm sun bathed the mountains and the like with brilliant color. The snow-capped peaks reflected in the deep blue of the water and I began to feel the inner warmth of serene, peaceful surroundings.

The tranquillity of the Great Creator's handiwork lay before me and the mountains and the little lake seemed to bid me welcome. The cares and frustrations of a busy life melted away. The gabble of the quietly feeding geese carried a note of peacefulness deep into my innermost being.

I felt joy flooding through me as I looked forward to at least two weeks of this peaceful life. The grandeur of the northland's finest scenery lay all around me in intense technicolor as I continued to drink in the beauty of nature in all her regal splendor.

Inch by slow inch, I rose onto my elbows. When my face was nearly level with the top of the grass blades, the old gander sounded the alarm with strident and frantic honking. The calm air was rent with the splattering roar and whistling of big wings beating hard to lift the geese into a maximum-effort takeoff. The wings beat with blurring speed as the big honkers lifted two or three feet into the air, then leveled off, flying low and fast across the lake as they picked up flying speed.

At the end of the lake, the loose formation banked into a tight climbing turn that reminded me of navy fighter planes climbing into combat. Less than one-half mile away, the gander led his flock into a final turn and flareout as they settled onto another small lake.

I rose to my feet and headed back to the old wagon trail, admiring the tremendous power of the wings of the Canadian goose and the thrilling beauty of the magnificent bird in flight. Swinging up the trail, I picked up my stride and felt my leg muscles loosen in the gradual climb. All around me, I heard the bird-like whistle of the little ground squirrels and, every few minutes, one would run ahead of me on the trail, then stop suddenly, and, standing upright, eye me with a suspicious look.

Their small bristle-brush tails stuck straight up like ra-dio antennas as they scurried ahead, warning others of the approaching intruder.

After a short lunch stop I continued the first day's climb, getting the feel of the trail under my feet and grad-ually becoming attuned to the activities around me. Not a human was in sight and the songs of robins and mountain thrush blended with the tuneful whistle of the ever-present ground squirrels, or parka squirrels, as they are called by Alaskans.

Small, sharp-eyed field mice peeped at me from behind stumps and deadfall, and an occasional snowshoe hare bounded away from his hiding place at my approach. As the late afternoon sun began to lengthen the shadows around me, I looked back down the trail and was sur-prised at the altitude I had gained.

Gazing high into the blue dome of heaven, I saw the sharp outline of an eagle as he wheeled and soared on silent wings, circling slowly on the updrafts, no sign of movement in his wings as he gained altitude over the val-ley. I envied his majestic beauty and freedom, and the eyesight that must have enabled him to see miles into the clear mountain air.

Ahead and far above me, I saw the sharp peak of Mt. Bona, lifting its spires well over sixteen thousand feet and, to the left and north, was the summit of Regal Mountain. Nestled between them lay the beautiful stretch of Russell Glacier and the Skolai Pass, which was my destination in the next few days. The top of Regal Mountain was over thirteen thousand feet high, but I knew I would not have to climb much over nine thousand feet to cross Skolai Pass.

Beginning to tire from the first day of walking, I found a small, level bench alongside a clear stream and soon had a bed of spruce boughs laid out under a rock ledge. The hot coffee from the crackling campfire tasted better than it had ever tasted before. I ate a light dinner and lit my pipe and sat watching the campfire, as evening shadows gathered softly around me, and the sounds of the little night creatures wafted quietly on the still air. I kept lis-tening for the howl of a wolf, but the only distant sounds were the soft sighing of the night wind through the pass and the occasional discordant yapping of coyotes.

I watched the glow of the rising moon over the shoulder of Mt. Bona; soon a full moon covered my little campground with soft light. My heart was full of peace. The quiet, serene night lulled my spirit and sleep soon came over me.

The following two days of climbing found me close to the pass, and nature continued to unveil constantly changing scenes of beauty. I came out on top of one shelf-like rock shoulder of the mountain, and stretching as far as my eyes could see were snow-capped peaks, dozens of them, marching across the rugged land like battalions of granite sentries—silent, unmoving, ageless.

The colors of rock strata amazed me and strong banks of green, gray, tan, and all shades of brown showed on the sheer walls, where nature had moved millions of tons of rock in some prehistoric convulsion.

Standing on the high outcropping, I saw the cool soft blue of Russell Glacier. Working my way across the foot of this relic of the ice age, I was shocked by the depth of some of the chasms and cracks in the ice. Sunlight filtered through the opaque ice with the cool, almost neon blue color found only in glaciers.

At the foot of the big glacier, the rocks and shale were worn smooth from countless ages of melting water and being rolled along by the glacier during the active stage of its long-past advance.

The milky gray color of the river flowing from under the glacier was typical of the runoff of several such small glaciers I had seen. I stared in awe at the thousands, or, rather hundreds of thousands, of square acres the glacier covered as it reached up between three mountains and spread almost to the tops of the blind canyons.

High among the peaks, clouds gathered around in rolling white cumulus, reminding me of a council meeting of the gods, with streaks of sunshine reaching down between the pillars to touch the great incline of the glacier. The shadows and highlights of the sunshine slanting down between the clouds and mountain peaks, coupled with the complete silence, made me feel I was in another world.

The grandeur of this wilderness gripped me deeply and I seemed to feel it plumb my soul.

The words of an old hymn came into my mind: "Then sings my soul, My Savior God to Thee, How great Thou art, How great Thou Art."

After drinking in this awe-inspiring scene for over an hour, I moved on down the trail, wondering how the old miners must have felt when they looked at this same scene. Having crossed the pass, I looked down into another valley, also surrounded by peaks and crags, and through the valley floor I saw the winding blue thread of the headwaters of the White River, which later crossed the Yukon Border and had its terminus in a distant delta.

Before leaving on my trip, I had heard Charley mention an old, long-abandoned gold mining camp that had been located somewhere along the trail across the pass. I began to watch closely for signs of a lost era, but the overgrown trail had yet to reveal any secrets of its past.

I found the old, rotted remains of a wooden wagon wheel, with its iron rim nearly disintegrated from rusting, and this whetted my curiosity.

The trail continued to descend through tall, handsome groves of aspen, white birch and spruce, and I welcomed the return of the friendly trees. I crossed a small creek churning with cold white water and continued on down into a dense stand of timber. Looking ahead, I detected a movement of something large in the trees, and I assumed it to be another moose, of which there were many in these parts.

A few steps further and the head and shoulders of a big eight-foot Toklat grizzly rose silently. The bear was standing on his hind legs watching me, his long dished face swinging back and forth in the shadows, trying to catch my scent.

I stopped, frozen in my tracks, and quietly slipped a cartridge into the chamber of my rifle, then eased the safety down into the firing position. I stood motionless, thinking of the tales I had heard of the short-tempered grizzly, and I remembered old Charley's advice that the grizzly was unpredictable but had no desire to associate with man. At a range of about one hundred yards, the grizzly looked plenty big and I knew his blinding speed could cover that distance in a few seconds, if he should charge.

I slipped three more cartridges between the fingers of my left hand, and with the four in the rifle felt I could stop him if necessary. The bear continued to test the wind and, catching the sudden man smell, let out a bawl and dropped to all four legs, traveling down the canyon at a full rolling gallop.

I realized I had been holding my breath, then heaved a sigh of relief. Dropping the three cartridges back into my jacket pocket, I set the safety on the rifle and continued on down the gradual decline.

Nearly a half mile ahead, I saw movement in the open grassy area, and through binoculars I saw the grizzly still rolling along with his peculiar gallop. Mentally I threw this at him: "You're doing fine, old bear. Just keep right on moving out."

Winding on down the trail, I began to see old pieces of boards and remains of old wagon parts, nearly unrecognizable from the ravages of time. These obscure signs of a bygone way of life showed me I was approaching an area that had seen the hand of man and I began to search the sides of the old trail more closely.

About forty feet ahead there was a movement on the trail. I stared in disbelief. Standing on their hind legs, two little parka squirrels stood facing each other, one with its front paws on the other's shoulders. The second squirrel was busily stuffing seeds into the mouth of the first squirrel. I stared for a few moments, then burst out laughing. The two little squirrels turned to look at me in surprise, then dropped down on all fours to scamper away in the underbrush.

As I came around a bend in the trail a fascinating scene unfolded before me. The grove of white birch and spruce trees spread out into a clearing, a sort of mountain pasture with tall grass waving in the breeze. Bright sunlight flooded the woods and illuminated the crumbling, rotting remains of four small one-room log cabins and one larger log building that may have been a bunkhouse or a roadhouse.

To one side of the larger log house were signs of what appeared to have been a corral, with rotting log poles lying in the grass. The poles seemed to have been built in the form of the ancient stake-and-rider style of fence. I stood in utter fascination, studying in detail the ghostly way station. Not a sign of recent habitation was visible, and the only sounds were the whistle of the ever-present parka squirrels and the soft sighing of the wind.

This was what I had been looking for, the old abandoned village Charley had heard of but never seen. I moved slowly in among the cabins, watching carefully for signs of bear, and saw many recent grizzly tracks interlaced with many moose tracks.

At the far end of the small group of cabins, a badger waddled off into the brush. Behind the old corral, on a small tree-shaded mound, was an old, rotten wooden cross standing in the grass. I moved in to investigate. The cross was made of hand-hewn boards, part of which had rotted and fallen away. But I made out the remaining hand-carved inscription: "Buck——" and the year 1898.

In front of the cross was a sunken place in the ground, three by six feet. Alongside this grave were signs of three more unmarked graves and one appeared to have been partly dug out by animals. I probed gently into the opening and saw the bleached bones of a human skeleton. The skull structure appeared to be that of an Indian or someone who had prominent cheekbones. Most of the teeth were gone from the skull, and I also found rotted remains of what probably was at one time a wool blanket or wool shirt.

I wondered what life had been like for these hardy pioneers, what had brought them to this faraway mountain glen, and what had caused their demise. Had they been stricken with disease or had they died from violence—either animal or human? As gently as possible, I slipped parts of two old boards across the opening in the grave, then covered the boards with as much dirt as I could push on them with my boots.

Lengthening shadows across the glen told me night and darkness would soon arrive. I scouted the area around the cabins again and found a grassy place for my camp and soon had a fire going. Hot bouillon and some food satisfied my hunger, and afterward I lighted my pipe and sat by the campfire, dreaming of the past and the people who had walked this trail. I imagined their hardships and pictured the determination that must have driven them relentlessly.

Like me, they must have answered the call of the wild, searching for adventure and a new life. I thought back over my own past and recalled with mixed emotions the years I had spent in law enforcement in a large city, and the suffering of others I had tried to help relieve.

I remembered the last sight I had had of my three little children, in Missouri, whom I might not ever see again. As they had done before, painful memories shot through my heart, and, again, I had to fight back tears.

The night wind whispered softly through the trees. Brilliant stars sparkled in the dark sky and hushed sounds of the little night creatures surrounded me. My thoughts moved back further in my own time, and I remembered my father saying grace at the table, his sturdy hands folded and his weatherbeaten head bowed in prayer. I recalled the thrilling beauty of the Ozark hills in autumn, and the gentle love of a beautiful woman.

The memory of the thundering power of a Pratt-Whitney aircraft engine at full throttle crossed my mind and the smell of salt spray blown across the flight deck of an aircraft carrier seemed real once again. My mind was filled with the peace and solitude of my present surroundings. I needed this quiet, and now I knew the deep fulfillment that comes with answering the call of the wild.

Climbing into my sleeping bag, I pulled my rifle close beside me in case of unwanted bear visitors, and sleep soon overtook me.

At dawn I quickly got breakfast out of the way and began a more thorough search of the old way station. The largest of the buildings contained old, rotted, and crumbling tables and chairs, all handhewn from spruce or birch. Stuffed into a corner was some old, yellowed, and disintegrating paper which looked as though it could once have been a newspaper. But the printing had faded away. The remains of two handmade bunks stood in one corner, with rotten strands of rope around one corner post.

In one of the smaller cabins I found two bottles half-buried in the dirt. One was made of white milk glass with a cut-glass stopper; it appeared to have been a medicine bottle. The stamp on the bottom was nearly illegible, but I was able to read the date: 1882.

The other bottle was brown colored, with a high neck that resembled a whiskey bottle of the one quart size, but without a stamp or date. Both bottles were carefully wiped clean of dirt, wrapped in an undershirt, and stored safely in my pack.

In one of the other cabins I found the remains of what appeared to have been a .44-caliber Henry repeating rifle. Its wooden stock had long ago succumbed to the elements and the steel barrel was crusted heavily with rust. Its brass receiver held less rust, but was corroded almost beyond recognition. With a stick I scraped away as much dirt and rust as possible, and then placed this ancient relic in my pack long with my other Klondike treasures.

A further search of the cabins revealed some rusted horseshoe nails, three narrow-gauge railroad spikes, some fragments of broken bottles, and a rusted table fork. I wrapped up the nails, spikes, and the fork and placed them in my pack.

I began to spread my search in a circle about fifty yards from the cabins and found what appeared to be another grave on the opposite side of camp from the others. Hidden in the weeds and grass were the rims and rotted wooden hubs of three old wagon wheels, and a few more pieces of scrap iron that could have come from an old freight wagon.

The remainder of that day and part of the following day I spent in prowling the lonely camp, and, all the time, my mind pondered its history. I knew my treasure was here, wrapped in the wilderness and mountains beside the lonely White River.

I felt a great satisfaction in that I had been permitted to walk into the past history of a great country and era and see and feel the treasures that Mother Nature had preserved for my visit.

Gratefully, I turned my back on the old way station and retraced my climb toward the pass. At the last turn of the trail, I stopped and looked back for a moment on the ghosts of the past. Then I resumed my homeward trek. Again, the peaks rose around me and I felt eager to return home and tell old Charley that I had found his Shangri-

La of the past and to show him the relics that would date back to his boyhood.

Four days later I stood at the end of the old abandoned airstrip, with a yellow marker panel stretched at my feet. Warm sunshine lay all around me and across the valley where I had started my trip on foot. Looking at my map, I estimated I had covered a little over one hundred miles in seventeen days; I felt rested and in excellent condition.

Off in the distance I heard the hum of an aircraft engine and the plane was soon turning onto the airstrip. I climbed into the plane, the roar of the engine providing background music for my thoughts as we headed for home.

12
Farewell to an Old Friend

The first time I had ever seen old Charley was on a cold, bright, winter day late in March of 1961. I had gone into a hardware store in Anchorage to buy some sections of stovepipe for my homestead cabin. Charley was working behind the counter, punching the keys of an antique adding machine. When I walked up to him, he looked up at me with a smile and said cheerfully, "Can I help you?"

He was the type of man one takes a liking to at first sight, and his appearance was typical of many Alaskan frontiersmen. He was short with a stocky build and his snow-white hair was neatly combed straight back. He wore the typical wool plaid shirt and wool whipcord pants with the sewn-in crease. His clear Scandinavian blue eyes looked straight at me. I liked his frank gaze.

I gave him my order, and we started talking about hunting, trapping, and homesteading and soon found we had many interests in common. When I told him about my current cabin-building project high in the Talkeetna Mountains, Charley informed me he had been a homesteader in Alaska since 1936.

Asked for his last name, he chuckled. "You couldn't pronounce it. I came from Finland, and even the Finns had trouble with it, so just call me Charley."

When I picked up the stovepipe and a few other items and started to leave, Charley told me to look him up again soon. I promised to go with him to visit his cabin when he had a few days off.

As it turned out, Charley's cabin was about two hundred miles northeast of Anchorage on the west shore of a lake hidden in the Chugach Mountains, at least thirty miles from the nearest village. The cabin was surrounded by a wealth of natural beauty: breath-takingly high snow-capped peaks, spruce- and birch-studded slopes, and a deep blue lake about five hundred feet from his front door. While we rattled and bumped along the rough trail toward it, Charley told me how he and his father had immigrated from Finland in 1934, traveling along on foot with several other herdsmen, and a herd of seven thousand reindeer to be delivered in Alaska under a contract to the United States Government.

He spoke of the long months on the trail, the hardships of the bitter winter months, the howling wind and biting cold, and the white-outs that strike terror into the hearts of seasoned outdoorsmen.

Then his face beamed and a big smile covered it. "But we made it okay, by golly."

His old jeep rattled on up the trail and I sat wondering what kind of courage and stamina allowed men to survive the unheard-of rigors and hardships of such a trip. I asked Charley how old he was. He chuckled again. "I don't know, son; I quit counting when I reached seventy-five, and that was several years ago."

I had guessed his age at about sixty-five and his excellent physical condition made him look even younger. We clattered to a stop at the end of the rough trail. Charley was the first to climb out of the jeep.

"Okay, another three miles on foot and we've got it made."

I felt like groaning when I looked at the two large packs of groceries which we had to pack in to the cabin, but Charley swung his pack up on his shoulders as though it were a toy. We picked up our rifles and started down the trail. The old man warned me to keep my eyes open as we were going to cross several grizzly trails, and I wished then that I had eyes in the back of my head.

The warm sunshine, the quiet beauty of the lake, and the cheerful whistle of little beady-eyed ground squirrels soon eased my worry about bears. When we reached the cabin, I slipped off my pack and stood gazing awestricken at the majesty of the surroundings. I told Charley he was living close to Heaven.

His smile was wide. "That's just the way I feel."

Charley's cabin was beautiful; it was made of peeled and hand-hewn spruce logs, and the fit of the doors, windows, and logs indicated expert craftsmanship. The shake roof was unlike any I had seen, secure and weather-tight, and the inside of the cabin was neat and clean. His hand-made shelves and cupboards were admirable.

The double-deck bunks were made of spruce poles and covered with bright Hudson Bay blankets, and the small Yukon stove was shiny black. The atmosphere of the cabin and its surroundings made me feel at home and I told Charley a person could stay here forever.

Again he gave me his big grin. "I do stay here every winter so I can do a little trapping and hunting. I work part-time in town once in a while when the mood strikes me."

After a week of paddling Charley's canoe around the lake, catching rainbow trout and grayling, dozing in the warm sunshine, cooking over an open campfire in front of the cabin, I really felt at home. We spent the mornings watching brilliant sunrises and sat in silence watching golden sunsets, then picked out navigation stars in the night skies.

During this week, old Charley and I formed a solid friendship; with his wilderness experience, he had much to teach me—little things I will always remember. His way with the small creatures and parka squirrels, for instance, was warm and friendly, and it was an education to watch the way they greeted him as one who belonged to their way of life.

On the morning we prepared to leave, I remarked that the smooth open pasture north of the cabin would make a good place to land my Piper Cub, if he should ever want to fly in. Charley shook his head.

"Nothing doing. If we make an airstrip here, every Tom, Dick, and Harry in the country will try to land here."

He grumbled about trouble with float planes on the lake during summer and ski-equipped planes in the winter;

after seeing the lonely beauty of the surroundings, I couldn't resist agreeing with him.

On the walk back to the jeep, Charley led the way down the trail and just after rounding a bend in the trail he stopped suddenly and held out his hand to signal me to stop. Looking ahead of the old man, I saw a large grizzly standing on his hind legs about seventy-five yards from us and I quietly eased a cartridge into the chamber of my old Winchester.

Charley's voice came back to me softly: "Don't shoot unless he charges."

We stood still, hardly breathing, and a chill ran up my spine. The bear's head swayed back and forth as he tried to get our wind, and soft growls rumbled deep in his throat. After two or three minutes that seemed like years, the big grizzly dropped down on all four legs, wheeled, and broke into his peculiar lumbering gallop up the side of the mountain. I started to breathe again.

Charley swung his rifle back over his shoulder. "Most of the time, those old boys won't bother you if you don't crowd them, but don't ever crowd one of them."

I had killed a grizzly the year before and had developed a healthy respect for them. But even with a .375 Magnum rifle, I still didn't like the idea of surprising one on the trail. I kept up a clattering conversation, therefore, with Charley until we reached the jeep.

During the next two years, I made several trips to Charley's cabin and we spent many pleasant hours together, snowshoeing his trapline, fishing in the lake, and moose-hunting during the golden autumn days. During his winter stays, I made frequent trips to his cabin to bring in his mail and groceries.

His needs were simple and he led the clean, carefree life of a true woodsman. He spurned the cities and towns and wanted only to live as he did, close to his beloved wilderness, with a few good friends with whom he could visit occasionally.

He seldom spoke of his youth in Finland and told me he was the only one left alive of his family. He had an old worn Bible, printed in his native tongue, and a faded, aged photograph of his mother and father dressed in their native costumes. Every Sunday morning, Charley took his old Bible down from its shelf, read for a while, then knelt in prayer beside his bunk.

He spoke of the wilderness as being "the art work of the Almighty," and he had a deep reverence for the beauties of creation and for the Heavenly Father who had given Charley his place here on earth.

About this time, I had traded my Piper Cub airplane and had gone into a partnership on a Cessna 180. I finally talked Charley into taking a plane ride on a calm summer day. As we lifted off the runway at Merrill Field in Anchorage, I saw his hands tightly grip the seat. He stared straight ahead. He was petrified.

I tried to put him at his ease. "Charley, don't worry. You're safer up here than you would be in that old jeep."

His head turned slowly and he stared at me intently. "Okay, if you say so."

He never did like flying; several times he said, "Those darn fool contraptions will get a man hurt."

One cold winter morning I sat in the Cessna at Merrill Field, waiting while the engine warmed up, and checked over the list of groceries tied down in the back seat. The box of groceries had a few extra goodies, since this would be Charley's Thanksgiving dinner. A few weeks before, we had installed wheel-skis on the Cessna for landing and taking off from frozen lakes and snow-covered bush strips. Now I planned to land on the lake in front of Charley's cabin and surprise him with a Thanksgiving dinner.

After an engine run-up and clearance from the tower, I lifted into the early dawn and headed northeast toward the Copper Valley and Charley's cabin. The bitterly cold outside air was calm, and the clear blue sky overhead promised a beautiful winter's day. A gold sun peeked over the horizon to make the deep blue sky lighten with the first rays of sunrise. Stretching far to the north, the Talkeetna Mountains turned from snowy white to deep rose pink as the mantle of first sunlight touched them.

To the south, the Chugach Mountains turned brilliant pink; to the southeast, in the far distance, the St. Elias Range with its great peaks turned from pink into bright yellow as the full light of sunrise drifted slowly down through canyons and crags.

Behind me, and far to the northwest, Mt. McKinley

and its companion, Mt. Foraker, towered over the skyline, crimson against the dark western sky. I wished this scene could last forever. The ragged, snow-covered peaks of Chickaloon Pass slipped by under the wing tips, and I set up a new course and heading that would take me directly to the lake in front of Charley's cabin. After a short time, I saw the lake below me and I throttled back, losing altitude.

After a long spiral across the lake, I flew low over the cabin to let Charley know he had company and as I passed over the cabin I noticed there was no smoke coming from the chimney. The only tracks in the new snow around the cabin appeared to be wolf tracks.

I circled around and made another low pass over the cabin, pushing in full climb power, so that he couldn't keep from hearing the engines. I circled again, and again made a low pass across the cabin. Still no signs of life.

I thought he might be out on his trap line, but his snowshoes were standing against the front of the cabin. I throttled back the engine and landed on the lake, which was still frozen and covered with nearly a foot of snow. I taxied up to the cabin and shut off the engine, climbed out, and put on my snowshoes, then walked up to the cabin door.

I shouted, "Charley, it's me, Dan! Are you home?"

The deep silence closed in around me and I studied the wolf tracks around the cabin. Now I was really worried. Something was wrong.

Again I shouted. "Charley?"

Again, there was no answer.

My first thought was that a wolverine might have moved into the area and caught Charley unaware. I put my right hand on the butt of my .44 Magnum pistol and with my left hand I slowly opened the cabin door.

The cabin interior was cold. The fire had gone out long ago. Looking at the lower bunk, I saw Charley wrapped in his sleeping bag with the bright red blanket over it. Moving over to the bunk, I looked down at my old friend, who appeared to be sleeping peacefully. With my fingers on the side of his neck, I searched for a pulse, but the cold, stiff body was evidence that his spirit had long since passed into eternity. Tears came to my eyes and I was filled with a heavy burden of sorrow.

Everything in the cabin appeared to be exactly as he always kept it—neat and orderly. Dishes were clean and the wood box was full; it appeared that he had died in his sleep. I pulled the blanket over his face and quietly closed the cabin door. The Cessna engine roared into life and I lifted off the lake for the short flight into Glenallen.

En route, I asked the FAA at Glenallen to have the state trooper meet me at the airport. I explained what I had found and the trooper told me that one of the local residents had visited Charley four days ago and he was not, at that time, feeling good. The trooper climbed into the Cessna, and we flew back to the lake and landed at the cabin.

After his investigation, the trooper asked whether Charley would have any preference for burial, and I answered that I didn't know, that Glenallen seemed as good a place as any. I took a long last look at my old friend, then we closed the cabin door and secured it with a wedge. The trooper said local arrangements could be made for the services.

We took off from the lake and I flew low over the cabin, rocking the wings in farewell to an old friend. I landed at Glenallen and let the trooper out, and I received his promise to take good care of old Charley and his possessions.

The Cessna lifted off the runway and I pointed its nose into the sunset and home. The crimson rays of the setting sun were filled with a deep loneliness and my heart ached for the old trapper who had passed away with no one near to comfort him, and few who knew or cared that he was gone. Recalling the many happy days I had spent at his cabin I was filled with nostalgia, but I still knew that old Charley had died as he would have wished—at home in the mountains, beside the quiet lake.

13
Moose from Every Angle

During my years in Alaska I have learned many things about moose and not all of the things I have learned are good, either. I have been chased by moose, kicked by moose, ignored by moose, insulted by them, and even run off the road by them.

I have observed them from every angle, upside-down, front side, broadside, backside, and from up in a tree looking down on them. However, the best view I have ever had of a moose is looking down on his remains sizzling in a frying pan, or broiling over an open campfire.

Countless times, I have seen a line of traffic on a highway stopped by a stubborn, haughty cow or bull moose standing in the middle of the road, absolutely refusing to move for any reason, even when confronted with a snorting, roaring, twenty-ton Kenworth Diesel truck.

In order to give the devil his due, I should say that no one can deny that a moose can read a calendar. During the winter, spring, and summer months, I could count moose on an adding machine. Then when hunting season arrives, *Pfffftttt!* Gone like a puff of campfire smoke on a windy night.

One week I drove out of Anchorage headed for our homestead seventy miles north of town. It is nestled at the end of a lovely two-mile-long lake in the foothills of the Talkeetna Mountains. From the Big Lake Highway, a gravel (sometimes) road winds up and down through the hills, across shallow creeks, through groves of white birch, aspen, and cottonwood, across tundra and muskeg, over hilltops and canyons, and at last, if you look quickly, there is a quick glimpse of a small cabin through the birch trees.

The winter snow, which was unusually heavy that winter, was melting fast and the warm spring sun beat down on the peaceful wilderness. Several times I shifted into low gear and let the Ford pickup growl its way across creeks filled over a foot deep with melting snow water. Plowed snowbanks on either side of the road were still deep and packed into the ditches. I saw several moose browsing in the willow thickets, scattered at random through the brush and heavy timber, but none was close enough to the road to cause any traffic problems. In the cab of the pickup I carried the usual wilderness equipment: a .44 Magnum pistol, regarded as standard life insurance by most Alaskans, enough food for the weekend, a rifle, a first-aid kit, flares, chains, cables, shovel, etc. The pickup, equipped with studded tires, also had a posi-traction differential, which is greatly favored in the rough back country, since neither rear wheel will spin unless the other does also. The emergency equipment was far from my mind as I drove along the road at about twenty miles per hour, ignoring all but the biggest ruts and mud holes.

Driving over a rise, I saw the road ahead drop down into a creek where the water was running fast, so I stopped and got out to look closer. I decided it was safe to cross, and then I drove on across. Water came up on the wheel hubs. I knew from experience the brakes would probably be wet, but would dry out in another mile or two. I continued on around a bend in the road, blissfully soaking up the spring sunshine.

Driving downhill past a dark grove of spruce and tamarack, I caught a sudden glimpse of a giant, dark brown mass leaping from the trees toward my right front fender. Instinctively, I slammed on the brakes.

The big bull moose kept coming like an express train as the wet brakes locked and the pickup slid to the right. The right side of the pickup hit the left side of the moose with a jarring impact, knocking the moose down and spinning the pickup around to the right. It skidded sideways into a ditch, coming to rest on its right side in four feet of snow.

The snow was piled up around the windshield; with the truck on its side, I couldn't see out. I didn't know where the moose was or whether it was dead or injured.

In an emergency situation like that, the first thought that flashes through a person's mind raced through mine: Is this damn thing going to catch fire with me inside?

After any accident, I knew only too well, a person should, if at all possible, get out of the car, plane, or truck as *quickly* as *possible*. Fire is a real and present danger. I'd known of too many instances in which people had been burned to death in wrecks.

Immediately, I turned off the ignition switch, unfastened my seat belt, and, pushing my feet against the seat and steering column, opened the left door and dropped down to the road.

I looked around and saw the big bull standing in the middle of the road about fifty feet away, madder than a wet hen. His ears lay back as he started his charge.

I jerked the .44 from its holster and fired four fast shots into the road in front of the brute, showering him with mud and gravel and making my ears ring from the terrific muzzle blast of the big pistol.

The moose skidded to a stop, then trotted back to the starting line. I swung the cylinder of the gun open, reloaded the spent shells, and looked up. He charged again. And again I blasted three or four shots into the ground at his feet, and, again, the moose skidded to a stop, this time about thirty feet away.

The hair stood up on his neck and the flattened ears told me I was in for a fight. Just as I snapped the gun open to reload again, the bull shifted into high gear and charged.

I looked frantically for a place to get out of the way, but the snowbanks were too wide to jump across and the muddy side of the pickup was too slick to climb; so I dove for cover under the left rear wheel of the pickup.

It was too crowded and close to the ground and the mud in my face soured my sweet disposition. I felt the front hoof of the big eighteen-hundred-pound bull graze my right hip, which stuck out from under the pickup.

I felt him thunder on past, showering me with more mud and water, and, looking under my elbow, I saw him stop in the road about fifty yards away. I crawled out from under the pickup and finished reloading the pistol while keeping an eye on the moose.

By this time I was fast losing my temper, and when I saw his ears go back again I thought, Okay, you darn fool, this is your last trip.

As the moose swung into his third charge, I carefully lined the pistol sights on his front shoulder. The blast of the gun was followed instantly by the smack of the big slug. The moose spun sideways, falling at the edge of the road, kicking and bellowing. I took three or four quick steps toward him, and another shot behind his ear stopped all signs of life.

I looked around to see whether the animal had a mate, but the sun-bathed woods were still and there were no signs of movement anywhere. There was an ache in my shoulder and arm from the bouncing in the pickup and my ears still rang from the pistol shots.

I looked down at my muddy clothes and wet boots. After making sure there were no signs of life in the moose, I took my skinning knife and cut the animal's throat to facilitate proper bleed-out of the carcass. One more look at the pickup told me a tow truck was a must, so I started the ten mile hike back toward the highway.

After four hours of slogging through the mud and wading the creeks, I felt tired and my temper still sizzled. I kept hoping someone would come by and give me a ride, but not a soul showed up on the long road.

I finally reached the highway and a passing pickup stopped at my wave. I opened the door and the driver looked at me. "Good grief, pal, what hit you?"

As we drove down the highway to the nearest telephone, I related the details of the moose war I had just won and the driver grinned, then broke out into loud peals of laughter.

He turned to me with tears in his eyes. "I'm sorry, buddy, I wasn't laughing at you. I was just laughing at that stupid moose."

About this time, my temper had cooled and I laughed

with him, thinking how silly I must have looked, trying to burrow under my pickup.

A telephone call soon had a wrecker on the way. Then I notified the state department of fish and game, so the moose meat could be cared for and given to an orphans' home. Late that night I arrived back home, muddy and tired, but happy to be alive.

Moose are regarded as a constant highway hazard in Alaska and I remember several years ago when, on a bright winter morning, I made a flight with a friend in my single-engine Piper Cub. We were cruising at about three thousand feet, parallel to the Richardson Highway. We were enjoying the sight of the pale winter sun on the white snow below, and the grandeur of the mountains off to our west. I looked down the long, lonely expanse of vacant highway and saw one solitary car ahead, traveling in the same direction we were.

About the same time, off in a draw to the west of the highway, I saw a large moose headed toward the highway with its long, swinging stride. I mentally calculated a collision course between the moose and the car, and it appeared they would both reach the same spot at the same time.

I started to open my mouth to comment, but my friend spoke first. "Hey. That's going to be close."

A few seconds later, the moose, which apparently had remained concealed from the driver of the car, leaped onto the highway and was struck broadside by the car. The moose rolled up on the hood of the car, and the car spun into the ditch, with the dead moose draped across the hood and windshield.

As the car spun off the road, I watched with shock as the driver fell out the left door onto the highway, rolled over and over like a rag doll, then lay still.

I spoke to my friend. "That looks pretty serious. That guy on the highway needs help."

I banked into a tight circle, climbing for altitude, and switched the radio onto the emergency frequency. We kept watching the driver, but no signs of life were evident.

I began to transmit on the radio: "Mayday—Mayday—Mayday. This is Piper Seven Niner Zulu. Can anyone copy this radio?"

After three unsuccessful tries on the radio, I looked up and down the highway for miles in every direction and saw no cars. With still no answer to my distress call, and no cars in sight, I decided to make a low-altitude pass over the accident.

Dropping into a tight forward slip, the plane lost altitude rapidly, and as we passed low over the scene, the driver, who appeared to be a dark-haired girl, raised slowly to one elbow and lifted a hand toward us.

Knowing the driver couldn't survive long in the twenty-below-zero cold, I considered the dangers of landing on the highway and then decided it was an "or else" case. With still no cars in sight, I cut the throttle, lowered the flaps, and turning into the wind gently touched down on the highway.

I cut the engine and stopped a safe distance from the driver. My friend and I soon found that she, a girl in her twenties, had suffered a broken leg and severe bruises and appeared to be in shock.

We cut willow poles from the roadside trees and tied them to the leg as splints. Wrapping the girl in one of our sleeping bags, we loaded her into the back seat of the plane. I told my friend to hold her head and shoulders tight in his arms and I opened the throttle to full takeoff power.

As we climbed smoothly away from the scene, I heard the girl groan in the seat behind me. I asked my friend how she was doing. "It looks like she's in deep shock."

Since we knew the nearest hospital was about thirty minutes' flying time across the mountains, I pushed the engine hard for maximum speed. Calling again on the radio, I received an answer from the nearest FAA station advising me that an ambulance would be waiting for us. Before long, we saw the girl safely put in the ambulance and headed for a hospital.

Most of the time a moose will run from a human, but the mother instinct of a cow with a calf will cause a sudden charge. I once came upon the scene of a highway accident in which a diesel truck and trailer had hit a moose head-on, and the truck and driver came out second best at the bottom of a canyon.

I can recall several stops on a train ride to Fairbanks when the engine had to nudge an obstinate moose off the tracks.

One conductor on a train ride told me a big moose would derail a diesel locomotive on occasion; knowing the temperament of a moose, I certainly wouldn't argue with him.

During mating season, a bull moose will charge anything that moves, including trains and large trucks. I have learned when driving down a road never to blow the horn at a moose, but just to wait until the brute moves of his own accord.

The front hooves of a moose are pointed and sharp as razors, and when attacking, a moose will strike forward with its hooves—one blow can cause instant death to a human.

Most Alaskans with bush experience regard a moose as just as dangerous as a bear, and twice as unpredictable. On the other hand, many a homesteader owes his life to the high nutritional value of moose meat. After a cold winter of hunger and hardship, the taste of a sizzling, savory moose steak or roast has no equal.

I think the homeliest sight I've ever seen is a newborn moose calf tottering alongside its mother on long, spindly legs, the small bony, awkward body struggling to stay on its feet. The gentle, tender love of a mother for its baby is evident even in an animal as large and ugly as a cow moose, as she gently nudges the calf into its first steps. She leans against the baby to help keep its balance, guiding it away from danger, and teaching it the art of survival.

I have seen a full-grown moose moving at a full run, and the smooth-flowing stride covers a lot of ground in a hurry. The stamina of these big animals is unbelievable and they seem to run just as fast up the side of a mountain as on level terrain. During my years of association with these magnificent animals, I have learned one lesson and that is to expect the unexpected when near them.

I have seen instances where people living in the bush have made pets of moose who were of a seemingly sociable temperament, and they have fed these pets by hand during winter seasons when food was scarce.

One time, on a hunting trip in the McLaren River country, I found the skeletons of two bull moose with the horns interlocked. It appeared they had starved to death because of this freak condition.

And I can't help but remember two winters ago, when a special antlerless moose hunt was permitted in the Palmer Flats area of the Matanuska Valley north of Anchorage, with a total harvest of some three hundred animals permitted in this hunt.

I drove up the Glenn Highway and saw cars parked for miles across the flats, and the sound of gunfire rippled across the valley like the Battle of The Little Big Horn. I stopped along the highway to watch the carnage and actually saw two hunters involved in a fist fight over who had killed a cow moose. With disgust and bitterness, I drove on up the highway, wondering what had happened to the beautiful state I loved.

Now, the Palmer flats are bare, and where once a herd of several hundred animals grazed there is only wind-swept tundra, bare of wildlife except for the occasional tracks of a lone coyote or badger. The wide prairies where the moose herds once roamed now stand silent and unused. The silence of the wide-open spaces is broken only by the occasional gabble of a flight of Canadian honkers or mallard ducks as they drop in for a rest stop.

14
Frustrated Bear Hunters

During my years of living in and near the Alaskan wilderness I have developed a philosophy which has proven more or less satisfactory in dealing with bears: I won't bother them as long as they don't bother me.

A black bear is a curious animal and is always hungry. With the inroads of civilization into his domain, he is inclined to become lazy and loves nothing better than to find a meal in a garbage pit or barrel. He has become a mechanical genius of sorts and has learned how to paw or pry off the most stubborn garbage can lid.

The animal is shy by nature and is nature's leading comedian, but in spite of his shyness he has proven quite capable of living close to man. I have seen numerous hilarious incidents of a black bear being caught in the act of stealing food from the camp of some luckless hunter and the surprised look on the bear's face is really worth a belly laugh.

On the other side of the coin, an unfortunate individual who finds himself caught between a mother bear and her cubs in a surprise situation is in for a lot of sudden grief—unless he can clear the area in a big hurry. When two bear cubs engage in a wrestling match, the resemblance to human children at play is astounding.

My new, outdoor-loving wife and I were spending a few spring days at the small cabin we had finished together at the end of a beautiful lake in the northern sector of the Matanuska Valley. Having worked hard all day at clearing stumps from the driveway, we were bone-weary, so we decided to climb into our camp cots and sleeping bags for a much-needed rest. For added ventilation, I had tied a section of nylon cord around the door knob, leaving the door open about four inches and held thus by the cord.

About 4:00 a.m., I was roused from a deep sleep by the banging and rattling of the padlock on the door hasp. I opened my eyes and vaguely saw the outline of a black snout poking through the opening. My sleep-fogged mind made me think this was the neighbor's old dog Rex, who had come for an early morning visit.

"Go on," I called out. "Beat it, Rex!"

The black snout only grunted. From her sleeping bag, my wife's mumbled voice came: "Can't you get up without all that banging around?"

By this time I was fully awake and caught the unmistakable smell of black bear. The rattling and thumping at the door continued, and I leaped from my cot to grab the .44 Magnum pistol and head for the door.

The black snout disappeared and I swung the door open in time to see a black bear cub ambling up the driveway, closely followed by its mother, who kept giving me dirty looks over her shoulder.

About a hundred feet up the driveway, the mother bear stopped at the left door of our pickup, then stood on her hind legs, paws on the side of the truck, and peered into the cab. Drizzling rain had made the side of the truck wet, and the cub, imitating his mother, stood up with his muddy paws on the left front fender.

Apparently trying to climb onto the hood of the truck, he was surprised when his front paws slipped from the fender. He turned a backward somersault, squalling like a spanked child. The mother and cub continued their unhurried journey up the driveway, while my wife and I shook with laughter.

A grizzly is an entirely different breed of bear. He is more carnivorous and is even more shy of the man creature. I have watched the grizzly numerous times as he goes about his daily activities, far from the roads and houses of civilization. He is absolutely fearless, but will usually try to keep a lot of distance between man and himself whenever possible. When injured or enraged, he is capable of moving with blinding speed, and one swipe of a mighty front paw can bring instant death to any man or animal so unfortunate as to be in the way.

Even at a distance, the grizzly can be easily distinguished from other species of bear by the hump-backed appearance of the front shoulders, and the long dish-shaped face. The Toklat grizzly is even more readily distinguished by the blond diamond-shaped patch across his front shoulders. The grizzly seems to stay in his own territory to a large extent, but may cover many miles during a hunting foray. During a moose-hunting trip on the McLaren River a few years ago, I watched two male grizzlies battle for territorial rights and the savagery of their attack on one another left me with a healthy respect for their speed and power.

There is a real challenge in hunting for grizzly. Mere man is forced to call upon all his ability as a woodsman in matching wits with this rugged animal, and a successful hunt brings deep satisfaction to the man who has matched wits with the grizzly and won.

Lady Luck sometimes seems to play a large part in a successful bear hunt, and when she decides to smile on a hunter there seems to be no end of the good things that will come his way. By the same token, when she decides to frown on a hapless hunter everything that can go wrong will. This is known as Murphy's Law in the wilderness.

I remember when my friend Major Carl Irby and I decided to go on a hunting trip for black bear, so that Carl could have a black bear hide for his living room, as well as some meat for his locker. At the time we started planning the trip, little did we know that Murphy's Law was already in effect and that our trip would not go as we intended.

With a three-day weekend ahead of us, we loaded our supplies and equipment into my Dodge Power Wagon and headed out of Anchorage for what we hoped would be a successful hunt. Carl had not been bear-hunting during the past four or five years and was looking forward to the wilderness trip and a few days of peace and solitude.

We decided to head for the Copper Valley country, where black bear are usually found in abundance. Success seemed practically guaranteed. After several hours of hard driving, we turned off the Richardson Highway south of the village of Copper Center, then drove back into the foothills of the Chugach Mountains to make our first night's camp.

Shifting into low-range gears and four-wheel drive, we drove up a seldom-used jeep trail, with the Dodge growling up the steep grades. We found a level plateau covered with gravel, moss, and cranberry bushes, and, looking to the east, saw a wide panorama of the Copper River Valley, deep-blue skies, and a backdrop of the wild, rugged Wrangell Range.

Towering over our heads was a rough, jagged mountain peak; through binoculars we saw the vivid white patches that were Dall sheep.

I kept reminding Carl that "this is bear country. Anytime now."

We parked the Dodge in the middle of the clearing and soon had a late supper cooking. The smell of coffee and hot soup put a real edge on my appetite, and we unrolled our sleeping bags in the back of the pickup.

Carl kept asking me, "Where are all these bear you were telling me about?"

"Keep your eyes open, partner. They are all around us."

While eating supper, we kept our eyes moving back and forth over the bushes around the clearing and up on the mountainside above us. Following supper, we relaxed and started cleaning up the supper dishes. We were putting pots and pans back in the grub box when we heard a rustling and saw movement in the nearby bushes. We promptly froze in our tracks.

The rustling grew more vigorous and without thinking, I shouted "Bear!" and we both made a mad, leaping scramble for our rifles. Both our rifle bolts slammed shut at the same time and we wheeled to face the noise, rifles at the ready. Within a few moments a large snowshoe rabbit hopped out of the bushes and stared at us with utter disdain.

Carl and I both let out our breath in a sigh. Carl snorted. "Some bear."

We both threw back our heads and laughed. As we crawled into our sleeping bags, Carl turned to me. "Be sure to wake me if any more of those twenty-four-inch bear show up."

He was still chuckling long after we had gone to bed.

I felt the cold mountain wind on my face and rolled over to look at my wristwatch, which showed 4:00 A.M. I nudged Carl and told him to roll out, that it was time to start hunting. At this time of year, the sun at 4:00 A.M. was nearly forty-five degrees above the eastern rim of mountains, and even in my sleepy condition I thought we should have been hunting at least an hour ago.

We were soon into our clothes and making quick work of a breakfast of instant coffee and beef jerky, followed by a big handful of raisins.

I spent the next fifteen minutes carefully scrutinizing the surrounding mountainside with my binoculars, but I saw only the wind passing over the grasses, reminding me of the wind in the wheatfields of my childhood.

We made our way slowly down the mountainside and back to the Richardson Highway. I told Carl about a canyon south of us along the Tiekel River where I knew bear had been sighted frequently, so we drove south down the highway, working our way slowly through the gorges and canyons.

We stopped frequently to survey the slopes and mountainsides all around us, but the only visible living creatures were the countless hordes of rabbits, and, in the distance, an occasional coyote or porcupine. Not far from Thompson Pass we came to the dark canyon I had told Carl about earlier, and we pulled off the highway to park on a promontory which commanded a view of the canyon and river bottom.

After locking the pickup, we slung our rifles over our shoulders and started down into the canyon. We worked slowly through the aspen groves and clumps of alder and spruce and found numerous signs of bear. The size and shape of the paw prints left no doubt that a large grizzly had taken over the canyon and had run off all the black bear.

Many of the old-timers I had talked to over the years had told me that when a grizzly moves into a territory, the blackies promptly move to a friendlier climate. When we had moved deep into the canyon, I realized we would not see any black bear here, and since the grizzly was out of season it appeared our foray into this dark glen would be fruitless.

Working by hand signals, I motioned Carl to start working a circle back to the pickup, and we started a swing to the right. I moved along the river bank and came to a wide place in the river where the water was slack and the current slow. Across on the far side of the river, I caught sight of movement and froze in my tracks.

The movement exploded into a beating of white wings as a slim, graceful trumpeter swan lifted into flight, his long slender neck thrust forward as the powerful wings picked up speed. The swan flew low along the surface of the water, then lifted in a graceful arc above the treetops, disappearing in the distance.

When we had returned to the Dodge, Carl and I held a war council and studied maps of the area. We considered the pros and cons of heading farther north into the McLaren River country, then finally decided to hunt the Edgerton Cut-off down the Copper Valley to the village of Chitna.

Leaving the Richardson Highway, we began the dusty trip to Chitna over endless miles of gravel road. We drove slowly, looking closely into the underbrush and timber along the way. Several miles of silent driving and looking later, Carl suddenly sat up straight.

"Stop. I see something."

I slammed on the brakes as Carl opened the door of the pickup and dropped to the ground with his camera in his hand. He walked slowly, step by step, toward the underbrush, signaling for silence. I eased out of the pickup and walked back a few feet to see what he was after and saw him fade slowly into the trees with his camera at the ready.

Several slow minutes passed. Carl moved gently ahead, taking each slow step in absolute silence. I saw him gradually raise the camera, then I heard a sound that sent a chill running up my back. Softly, but clearly, through the trees came the "urk-urk-urk" of a cow moose giving the danger signal to its young.

At the same instant, Carl looked around me and patted his hip, the sign for back-up with a gun. I wheeled and grabbed my gun belt off the seat of the Dodge and started for Carl and saw him backing toward the road, staring intently at something ahead of him.

Just beyond Carl I saw the shape of a big cow moose moving slowly and stiff-leggedly toward him, her ears laid back flat and the hackles on her neck standing up. Just as Carl reached the edge of the road, the moose broke into a full charge, and I shouted: "Run for it, Carl!"

Carl ran toward me, with the moose coming faster, and I pulled the .44 Magnum from its holster when it began to look like Carl wasn't going to make it to safety. Just as I put the sights on the huge animal's front shoulder, the moose slid to a stop in the gravel, and I heard Carl pull his rifle from the right side of the cab.

The moose walked back and forth across the road and started to make another charge. About twenty feet from the back of the pickup, the cow moose stopped again, then turned and slowly walked into the brush at the edge of the road. She had walked into the brush, toward her twin calves, before it dawned on me that I had been taking pictures with my camera instead of keeping the gun pointed at the animal.

I turned to Carl. "Did you get your pictures?"

He grinned. "I don't remember. I was too busy getting out of the way."

Our laughter was a little nervous as we continued our slow trip down the road to Chitna.

Arriving in Chitna, we bought gas for the pickup and ate lunch, then passed the time of day talking hunting and fishing with the proprietor of the combination service station and country store. He dimmed our hopes somewhat by telling us that black bear had been scarce in the valley that spring, but he thought we might have better luck up north in the Glenallen area.

We drove out of Chitna headed for Glenallen, discussing our bad luck as we drove along. Coming to a wide turn-out on the high mountain road, I pulled the Dodge off the road. We climbed out and walked up a small incline; spread before us was an awe-inspiring view of the Copper Valley. The river wandered across the valley for miles, and to the north Mount Sanford and Mount Wrangell raised their magnificent snow-capped ramparts into a deep blue sky. The pure white of the snowy summits had started to turn pink in the first blush of sunset, and far up the valley the shadows deepened into purple and gray.

We stood in silence, gazing across the beautiful valley, and drank in the peace and contentment of the silent wilderness. In every direction we saw nothing but mountaintops, and to the east the stark, frozen beauty of the Wrangell peaks lifted in broken, jagged spires into the heavens.

I saw the high summit of Mount Bona, where, a few years back, I had spent three wonderful weeks hiking and camping in solitude, alone in the vast wild beauty of the great land. After nearly an hour of meditation, Carl and I drove on down the road, each wrapped in our own thoughts. He and I both felt the same after such a tremendous mountain-top experience; words were unnecessary and superfluous.

We were silent as we drove for several miles. Then I suddenly remembered a small lake off the side of this road, and I soon found the turn in the road I remembered. I told Carl about the small lake hidden in the trees, so we stopped along the road and I started back through the trees to look for any bear that might be around the lake.

About twenty feet from the road, the underbrush became so thick I couldn't see where I was going. I had just dropped down off a small ledge when the world erupted ten feet in front of me. I had nearly stepped on a moose calf lying on its side in the heavy brush, and the cow moose standing over it lunged at me.

The shock and surprise caused an instant reaction in my feet. I cleared the small ledge in one leap. I could feel the big cow right behind me in full charge and fear put speed into my legs. In four or five big leaps, I was clear of the brush and when Carl saw the look of fear on my face he jerked his rifle out of the pickup and swung it to cover me.

I covered the distance to the pickup in record time and slid to a stop in a shower of gravel. I grabbed frantically for my rifle. Carl was laughing.

"She's gone now."

I looked around and the cow was nowhere in sight. I stood there panting for breath, and Carl waited a minute. "Well, old buddy, turnabout is fair play."

A full-grown cow moose stands nearly six feet high at the front shoulders and averages over fourteen hundred pounds; the thought of being trampled by such a huge animal made a chill run up my back.

I turned to Carl. "Say, it just dawned on me that we're right in the middle of the moose calving grounds. Let's get out of here."

"Suits me. Let's get rolling."

Late evening found us north of Glenallen and approaching Gakona Junction. We found a quiet, secluded campground under some tall spruce trees and soon had the sleeping bags unrolled. We were both tired and soon fell asleep.

During the night, I thought my bed had gotten awfully hard and discovered my air mattress had developed a leak and gone flat. Fatigue overcame discomfort and I was soon back to sleep.

While I was dreaming about a beautiful sailboat on a calm Pacific Ocean, a big, nasty mosquito took aim at the end of my nose and its bite woke me. I looked at my watch and saw it was 3:00 A.M. My nose itched and my back hurt from the steel bed of the truck.

I nudged Carl. "Listen, buddy, I can't sleep. Let's get out of here and go hunting."

Carl rolled over and stared groggily at me. "What are you, some kind of hoot owl?"

I climbed out of my sleeping bag and soon had the coffeepot bubbling. The smell of hot coffee brought Carl fully awake. While eating breakfast, we talked of several places in which to hunt and finally decided to hunt off the highway back toward Anchorage, over two hundred miles away.

We headed slowly down the highway and stopped in Glenallen for gas. The service station attendant told us that there were black bear all over the place.

Carl muttered, "Yeah, where have I heard that before?"

We looked at each other and guffawed. Several miles on down the highway, we passed Gunsight Mountain Lodge and turned off on a side road which wound back up into the foothills of the Talkeetna Mountains. To the west, we saw Sheep Mountain and to the southwest stood the dark gorge marking the pass where the Glenn Highway wound beside the Matanusky River toward Palmer and Anchorage.

On the side of Sheep Mountain, our binoculars brought several bands of Dall sheep into focus, and we saw the lambs climbing among the rocks and crags with the ewes. Swinging our glasses around to the wide canyon stretching northward, we began a systematic search of the terrain for any signs of black bear. In spite of about twenty or thirty minutes of searching, we had seen only a lone cow moose, bedded down, and two lonely coyotes loping off into the distance.

We drove along the highway through Chickaloon Pass and a sudden idea hit me. I told Carl about a small lake I knew of where numerous black bear had been sighted; it was a place where I had taken two black bear in years past. Coming out of the pass and dropping down into the Matanusky Valley, we turned off the highway and wound far back into the Talkeetna Mountains over a rough gravel road into a sparsely populated section.

I told Carl: "If we are going to score, it will certainly be here."

Topping over a small rise, I slowed down and shifted into a lower gear, both of us straining our eyes forward and into the brush. We came around a sharp curve. I slammed on the brakes and stared in utter disbelief.

For over one hundred yards ahead of us the narrow road was clogged with a maze of cars parked in every direction, blocking traffic, and the air was full of the yapping, barking, and howling of all shapes and sizes of dogs. At the edge of the small lake stood a man with a shotgun, while nearby another man was periodically releasing ducks from a crate, to be shot and dropped into the lake for the dogs to retrieve. I looked at Carl in disgust and we turned around in the road and retraced our route.

Here in a secluded part of the wilderness, we had stumbled into retriever field trials—and the last thing we were searching for was a crowd.

I sighed. "To heck with it. Let's go on home."

Carl was silent awhile, then he agreed. We headed down the highway into Anchorage.

Upon arrival at home, we were subjected to much good-natured kidding from our wives, who casually remarked something to the effect that the "bear hunters came home bare."

Carl and I spent the following day sorting and cleaning our equipment and laying plans for another hunting trip later in the year.

That evening the phone rang, and my neighbor up at the lake asked where I had been. I told him about our unsuccessful bear hunt.

Over the phone he gasped. "Good grief, man, why don't you stay home once in a while? A big black bear has been hanging around your cabin for the past week or so."

Was Murphy's Law in effect that trip?

15
Avalanche!

The headlights of the Plymouth station wagon pierced the gloom of a bitterly cold winter morning; I saw the Seward Highway winding away, climbing upward toward the summit of Turnagain Pass several miles ahead. Off to my left was a canyon well over a thousand feet deep in places; to my right the headlights picked out the jagged ribs of the mountain which rose in nearly vertical terraces.

The highway was covered with a polished sheet of black ice, and driving required my utmost attention. My eyes burned from staring intently ahead and I kept trying to relax my aching shoulder muscles, sore from the hours of tense driving already behind me. I had driven this route many times in the past years under both winter and summer weather conditions, and two or three times I had personally seen the horrible results of one instant of inattention while driving on glare ice. Even the tiniest wrong move on my part would send the station wagon tumbling end over end into the canyon on its final ride.

About a week before, I had received an invitation from some friends in Seward to spend a week of my winter vacation visiting with them. They were a typical Alaskan couple—friendly, warmhearted, and generous—and I knew a week with them would be filled with pleasure. They both held the same love of the wilderness that I did, and I felt sure our first experience would be a rabbit-hunting trip on snowshoes on the back side of their eighty-acre tract of land just to the north of Seward.

I also looked forward to the evenings in front of their fireplace with its crackling log fire, and I could almost smell the moose steaks cooking. In the back of the station wagon, I carried a large box of good things to eat as a gift for their hospitality.

Along with the box of edibles was the usual survival equipment: a down-filled sleeping bag, first-aid kit, shovel, flares, chains, and a big game rifle. In the glove compartment rested a Colt Woodsman .22 pistol with several boxes of extra cartridges, an item carried by many Alaskans for the purpose of collecting rabbits and ptarmigan for a tasty evening meal. I wore a heavy wool shirt and pants, knee-high mukluks, mittens, and a down-filled, hooded parka, just in case of mechanical failure in the thirty-below-zero cold.

The light of dawn filled the canyon and the rocks and the snow-capped mountain peaks all around me separated themselves from the shadows of night. Trailing wisps of blowing snow chased ahead of me up the highway, driven by a moaning wind that swept the icy ridges and stands of black spruce trees. In the past weeks, the snowfall had been unusually heavy on the Kenai Peninsula and both Anchorage and Seward had received more than their share.

As the station wagon made its way slowly to the summit of Turnagain Pass, the morning sun touched the peaks high overhead and turned them into pastel shades of soft pink and lavender. I came to a wide place that had been plowed out along the edge of the highway and pulled off the road, clear of traffic. Climbing out of the wagon, I yawned and stretched, and the searing burn of the bitter wind on my face jerked me into instant alertness.

After five or six knee-bends, I leaped back into the warmth of the car, fully awake and on edge. A cup of coffee from the big stainless steel aircraft thermos bottle warmed me and the thought of good times ahead added to my inner glow. Looking forward and behind, I eased back onto the highway and started the gentle descent down the long mountain grade toward Seward, over forty miles distant. Little did I know or even dream what the next few hours would hold.

After passing Summit Lake, the highway twists and

turns as it lowers gently into the canyon at the head of Kenai Lake, where a highway junction suddenly appears out of nowhere. The Seward Highway bends easily left at the junction, while the right fork of the road leads on to Kenai and Homer, towns on the Kenai Peninsula. As I neared the junction, I casually glanced up at the high mountain peaks ahead and on both sides of the junction. Something unusual caught my eye. I noticed what appeared to be a thread line running completely across the face of the snow mass on the mountain wall about one mile ahead of and above me. A second glance at the horizontal thread line showed what appeared to be small curling puffs of snow. The thread-like line had widened slightly and now spread across the entire face of the mountain.

It dawned on me with a shock that the thread line was widening and the entire side of the mountain seemed to be moving slowly downward into the canyon. A chill shot up my spine and one word flashed into my mind: AVALANCHE!

Watching for a moment, I decided the snow mass would cross the highway ahead of me. I thought of a big diesel truck I had passed thirty minutes earlier and knew it would be along very soon, with all its massive weight. Easing to a stop, I slammed the Plymouth into reverse and turned to look backward, backing up the icy highway as fast as I could maneuver the wagon.

About one-fourth mile behind me, I saw a curve in the road over which I had just passed. I stopped in my own traffic lane, turned on the left turn signal for a warning blinker, then grabbed two red flares from the kit behind the seat. As I started to walk back up the highway, I heard the bellowing of the Jacobs brake on the big diesel truck, and I frantically yanked the cap off one of the flares, then struck the igniter hard.

The blinding red flare burst into life just as the truck appeared around the curve, and I swung the flare back and forth in the old railroad signal meaning "wash-out," or "shut down your engine." I heard a toot on the air horn of the truck, then dropped the flare on the center line of the highway. The big diesel eased to a stop and the driver leaned out the cab, looking over my head.

He muttered and breathed heavily, then came out with:
"My God, look at that!"

I turned in time to watch the big avalanche pick up momentum. A tremendous boiling cloud of loose snow lifted into the sky and, pushed by the raw wind coming up the canyon, drifted toward us. The giant avalanche roared downward toward the bottom of the canyon, with a fine wave of powdered snow traveling horizontally across the bottom of the canyon, spreading outward from its source like the ripples on a pond.

As the wall of finely powdered snow approached us with express train speed, the truck driver shouted, "Here she comes!"

Without thinking, I yanked the hood up on my parka and turned my back on the approaching shock wave. I felt a hard shove from behind that knocked me to my knees. With a giant "WHOOSH!" the shock wave passed. Then the air was filled with a twilight haze of finely powdered snow.

All around us was an eerie silence, except for what sounded like a roar of a violent windstorm down at the bottom and far end of the canyon. The haze of snow around me cleared gradually and once again sunlight filtered down through the peaks and crevasses.

Looking up at the side of the mountain that had just recently been smooth with new-fallen snow, I saw only a ragged, torn, and jumbled pathway with the bare rocks and pinnacles of the mountainside exposed to the sunlight. An entire wall of snow, nearly one thousand yards across, had slid down into the canyon and covered the highway.

At this point the truck and my station wagon were about one half mile back from the avalanche. The truck driver suggested we drive closer to see how much of the highway had been blocked, so we started our engines and drove slowly toward the blocked section of the highway.

About one hundred yards back from the wall of snow, we stopped. The truck driver and I each lit two red flares and placed them across the highway behind the truck. We walked up to the wall of snow that blocked the highway and I stared in amazement.

The snow across the highway appeared to be over twenty feet deep, stretching past the roadway and down into a creekbed nearly three hundred yards past the road. Sticking out of the snow mass were large tree trunks twisted like pretzels, and small trees that had been stripped clean of all bark and branches—looking strangely like the scattered bones of a prehistoric monster.

Mixed in with the shattered tree trunks were rocks and boulders of all sizes. The enormous size of the avalanche and the obvious evidence of its terrible destructive force left me speechless. I worried about the possibility of another snowslide in the area and took a pair of binoculars from the station wagon and scanned the peaks in the vicinity of the nearby mountains.

Two other cars pulled to a stop behind the truck, and two men walked up to stand beside the truck driver and me. One of them, a grizzled old-timer who lived in the area, seemed to think there was no immediate danger from any other slides in the vicinity, so I breathed easier. The old-timer said that Moose Pass wasn't very far down the highway past the avalanche, so he decided to go across the blocked area and see whether anyone had stopped on the other side.

After about twenty minutes he came back across the massive pile of snow and told us that a car had gone back to the highway department garage at Moose Pass to call for the big rotary snow plows. A short time later, we heard the roar of diesel engines coming down the highway and a big truck with a rotary snow plow on the front lunged repeatedly at the mass of snow. The plume of snow from the rotary arched high into the blue sky as the big truck ate away at the pile of snow blocking the roadway.

A large bulldozer arrived on the scene and pushed trees, limbs, and boulders off to the side, helping the snow plow eat its way through the pile. During a lull in the roar of the big engines, I heard diesel equipment working on the far side of the blocked area. After watching the heavy equipment work for over four hours, I once again saw the highway cleared for passage. Driving through the recently opened slide area, I looked at vertical walls of snow nearly twenty feet high alongside each shoulder of the roadway.

Most avalanches in Alaska occur far back in isolated, lonely ramparts of mountain ranges which are seldom, if ever, viewed by man, and only then by the bush pilots who patrol the remote regions. However, a part of the Seward Highway between Anchorage and Portage is built alongside a high mountain which rises abruptly out of the Turnagain Arm of Cook Inlet, and this section of highway is the scene of frequent avalanches which, combined with heavy snowfall and certain wind and temperature conditions, sometimes blocks the highway and adjacent railroad tracks.

Signs along the highway warn of avalanche danger and scars on the mountainside and highway guard rails attest to the mighty, ponderous force of thousands of tons of snow traveling down the mountains at express train speed.

Most Alaskan motorists who have become acquainted with mountain driving have learned to keep a wary eye on the upper slopes for the telltale hairline ridge across the face of a slope accompanied by the small, curling clouds of snow which mark the start of an avalanche. A driver who is keeping a sharp eye out ahead at a distance of one mile, or about forty-five degrees to the line of the road, can usually have time to brake his car to a stop, turn around in the road, and beat a retreat. By staying alert, a driver may be able to spot danger in time to warn other motorists and possibly avoid a tragedy.

Ski patrolmen, who are trained to spot potential avalanche conditions, patrol the mountain slopes of the nearby ski resorts, giving first aid to injured skiers and assistance to new skiers. At the same time, their sharp eyes roam the peaks and slopes, ready to sound a warning if dangerous conditions develop.

One winter I watched a forest service officer and ski resort personnel dislodge a heavy snow build-up which had become an avalanche hazard. Early in the morning, before the slopes were opened to the skiers, a 75-mm. recoilless rifle was set up and its muzzle trained on the exact spot where an avalanche would soon have started.

A tremendous flash of fire erupted from the back of the long-barreled rifle, accompanied by an ear-splitting crack as the gun discharged. A few seconds later, there was a puff of snow high up on the side of a snow-covered slope, and in a few more seconds I heard the rolling boom of the high-explosive charge and saw a long crack appear across the snow on the slope.

The slow first movements of the white tide were deceptive, and it seemed like a long time before the great mass of snow picked up speed and the big, boiling cloud of loose snow rose up into the sky. Falling harmlessly into a wide bowl of a canyon, the avalanche broke up and the great wave of snow came to a slow stop, its danger checked.

One veteran ski patrolman I talked with told me that persons caught in the path of an avalanche were taught to remove their skis or snowshoes quickly, and ride the surface of the snow wave with a breast-stroke swimming motion. The greatest danger, of course, is that of being buried under the snow, with suffocation a possible result.

Another ever-present problem during bitterly cold weather is the danger of frostbite, and the attendant suffering from exposure. Around Anchorage and the Matanuska Valley extremely severe conditions are seldom encountered, but many winter weeks will show a -35- to -45-degree reading in parts of the valley. Right now, as I write, the thermometer on my back porch shows twenty-eight degrees below zero and the wind is blowing at twenty-five miles per hour with gusts up to thirty-five mph. This temperature, coupled with the wind, produces a chill factor equal to about eighty-four degrees below zero.

A person who must be outside under these conditions has no choice but to dress with the proper type of clothing, or suffer the consequences. Since I am on call at all hours of the day or night, I have learned to keep heavy clothing at the ready.

Some of these items are a matter of personal choice, but for my own use I have found the following items necessary: quilted, down-filled long underwear, heavy wool shirt and pants, two pairs of heavy wool ski socks worn under knee-high shoe pacs which have three-fourth-inch thick wool felt liners, a quilted vest, a goose-down parka with a parka hood lined with wolf or wolverine fur, and, finally, double-lined fleece and leather-shell ski mittens.

Many people prefer the fish-net-knitted underwear, which is also very warm and comfortable. If a person has to be outside for long hours under severe conditions, one thing becomes extremely important: sweating must be avoided at all costs, since it rapidly lowers body temperature and can cause the onset of frostbite and exposure, with possible fatal results.

Frequently, city and state police find the bodies of exposure victims, frozen stiff. Research has proved that the consumption of alcoholic beverages in excess will speed up death from exposure under extreme conditions.

To prevent frostbite of the feet, it is necessary to wear footgear that is not too tight and extra wool socks, changed twice daily, become a must. When my partner and I are on a hunting trip in bitter weather, we keep a close watch on each other's nose and chin for the first telltale gray-white spots. Should these appear, we warm the affected places with the palm of a bare hand and we change hands frequently.

We have learned that the quickest way to hold off frostbite and exposure is to stop and rest frequently and build a campfire.

Under emergency conditions, I can put my partner's frozen foot under my armpit, next to the skin, and thaw it out. Among old-time Alaskans, it is a fairly common thing to meet those who have lost one or more fingers, toes, or feet from frostbite and freezing.

Deep in the interior of Alaska, temperatures have been recorded officially at eighty-six degrees below zero, and during the dead of winter temperatures at minus fifty degrees are common at Fairbanks. These temperatures take their toll on machines as well as men. An easy way to tell newcomers to the State of Alaska is to look for the ones whose cars repeatedly fail to start. Most Alaskans install a tank-type hot water heater in the engine cooling system, with a plug-in cord for a one-hundred-ten-volt outlet outside the house. An electric hotplate under the battery is also helpful and an engine tuneup becomes a must, unless one wishes to walk to work.

Even though the above notations concerning cold weather may seem unpleasant, I have found the winters in Alaska to be every bit as pleasant and rewarding as the summers. Nature turns the countryside into a wonderland of beauty, and I have found nothing so thrilling as a cross-country ski tour with a camera. Wind is a rare thing in the Matanuska Valley, and on windless days the squeak and squeal of dry powdered snow underfoot is a satisfying sound.

The short days of winter are made pleasant by a gathering of friends around a warm fireplace, and the evenings pass quickly when livened by friendship, light-hearted conversation, and song. The true Alaskan will come to treasure the winter season as one of the many moods of the great northland. I count myself fortunate to be included among those who have found their permanent home under the Aurora Borealis.

16
Fishing for Fun around Alaska

Not all phases of life in Alaska are serious. There is nothing a frontier Alaskan likes better than a practical joke or a good belly laugh.

Many of us around Anchorage have heard about one old fellow who had lived in Alaska for many years and who had, for some time, insisted on driving his older-model car instead of thinking about buying a new one.

He left Anchorage one day for a trip and, after driving many miles north on a major highway, he had a flat tire. Pulling onto the shoulder of the road, he walked around the car and opened its trunk.

He pulled the spare tire out of the car and laid it on the ground so he could get at the jack to jack up the rear end. As he knelt beside the flat tire, he glanced toward the front of the car and noticed that its hood was up. Walking to the front, he saw a stranger rapidly working to remove the battery and loosen the generator and carburetor bolts.

The stranger looked up. "You can have the back half. I get the front half."

One evening a special social occasion found me dining at one of Alaska's finest restaurants. It was elegantly appointed, with crisp white tablecloths on handsome oak tables, and real silver service gleaming in the pale candlelight. Massive overhead chandeliers spread a soft glow over tables and diners, mostly couples enjoying the intimate semi-darkness.

A maître d', dressed in formal clothes, guided late-arriving guests to their tables with befitting dignity and aplomb.

The restaurant was nearly filled when I glanced up in time to see an elderly lady enter. She was gowned in what appeared to be European lace of some heirloom style. Alone, she walked, her head held high in her lady-like dignity, behind the headwaiter to her table.

After she had been seated, she surveyed the surrounding diners with a haughty stare and ignored the printed menu which had been carefully placed before her. When a cocktail waitress approached the guest's table, the waitress was abruptly dismissed with curt words indicating her services were not needed. From her Teutonic accent, I judged the elderly woman to have had a German origin.

Finally, settled comfortably in her chair, she picked up her menu and began to scan its contents. She held it close to her eyes, moving it back and forth as she tried valiantly but unsuccessfully to focus her eyes on the richly embossed pages.

Several minutes of frustrated menu-staring went by. Defeated by the candle-lit darkness, she raised her head and turned to look around the entire room. Her gaze riveted on the bright lights evident near the kitchen steam tables in a distant corner of the restaurant.

Rising from her table, she headed for the kitchen, striding with the determination of a warrior marching into battle. She stood in the brightly lit arena of kitchen lights and read slowly down the pages of her menu. She was soon surrounded by a group of waitresses, the chef, and the headwaiter. The chef was obviously shocked that anyone would be so brash as to invade his domain and when the headwaiter asked whether he could be of service, the little old lady subjected him to a blistering tirade of her opinions of a restaurant which was too cheap to buy a few light bulbs so its guests could read the menu.

She delivered a stinging tongue-lashing flavored with a strong German accent. And then the little lady returned to her table with an air of ruffled dignity. Needless to say, she was given better service during the remainder of the dinner hour than was anyone else. I watched the faces of the other diners and saw many smiles of admiration turned her way. Secretly, I smiled, too, with respect for her courage.

Another old person I enjoyed was a trapper and miner who had spent most of his time living alone in the mountains of Alaska. He spent his days in a never-ending search for the elusive mother lode of gold that lives in the dreams of every old miner.

In a downtown cafe in Anchorage one day, I had coffee with him. He casually remarked that he had never been flying and would "sure like to take a ride in one of them flying machines." I told him I had a Super Cub at Merrill Field and would be more than happy to give him a ride, so he could see the sights from the air. The old fellow's face lit up in a smile. "I sure would be grateful."

In the plane, I removed the rear control stick and strapped him into the back seat. We were soon lifting from the runway into the bright afternoon sunshine. Making a few slow turns and banks, I pointed out several familiar landmarks, then turned northward to fly up the Matanuska Valley.

Looking back over my shoulder to see how the old man was doing, I saw his right hand in a tight grip on the back of my seat and his other hand firmly clamping his battered old hat onto his head. I kept up a conversation to try to relax him.

Finally I heard his slow dreamy voice say, "Boy, you sure can see a far piece up here."

We flew along in silence for a while. Then I felt a tap on one shoulder. I turned my head and he asked, "Say, son, jist how fast are we going, anyhow?"

I looked at the airspeed indicator. "We're flying about ninety-two miles per hour."

He thought for a second. "Well, son, you don't have to speed jist on my account."

It was different, however, the day a friend yelled to me to "stop the boat!"

Van Stewart was one of the few men with whom I really enjoyed fishing trips. While not exactly the most expert fisherman myself, I took great delight in watching Van go through the mystic ritual of selecting the proper rods, reels, fishing line, flies, plugs, and other numerous items to fill a tackle-box. Van had the typical All-American look and you could see the laughter in his eyes, even when his face wasn't covered with his wide easy grin as he surveyed his fishing equipment.

A man of about average height and build, he was typical of many frontiersmen in his care not to waste words. Conversation came easily for him, but he just wasn't the gabby type. He did, however, love practical jokes, and he could take them as well as dish them out.

We had planned a five-day fishing trip out of the seaport town of Seward, using my twenty-one-foot fiberglass-hulled boat with its twin outboard engines. We wanted to fish down the eastern shore of Resurrection Bay, then move on over toward the numerous small islands that lie between Montague Island and the mainland.

Having heard many tales of the unpredictable nature of the wind and waves in Resurrection Bay and the surrounding waters, I watched weather forecasts a week ahead of time. The evening before our departure, Van came over to my house and we spent several hours going over our equipment, checking each item off a list we had prepared earlier. After attaching the boat and trailer to the back of my pickup-camper, we drove to a corner service station and had the gas tanks filled on the pickup and the outboard motors, then filled the four long-range reserve tanks stored in the stern of the boat.

Just before dawn on the following morning, I drove up to the front of Van's house and tooted the horn. A few minutes later Van stumbled out his front door, rubbing sleep from his eyes and carrying a cardboard box under one arm.

He crawled into the cab of the pickup, mumbling, "You've got a lot of guts waking a guy up at this hour of the day."

"Well, pal, you can't catch fish with your head stuck under a pillow."

I eyed the box on his lap and waited for him to say something about it. Instead, he pulled one flap open, slipped out a piece of paper, and started trying to read it with the aid of the dashboard lights. My curiosity got the best of me.

"What's in the box, anyway?"

He stared at me a second. "For your information, friend, this is a life belt, complete with carbon dioxide cartridges."

"Now I like that! What's the matter, you got no faith in my boat?"

"Buddy, I don't care if you've got a battleship on that trailer. This belt goes with me whether or no."

"Let me put your mind at ease. There are six kapok life preservers in that boat, and any one of them will hold you up."

"I don't care. I'm taking my life belt, anyway."

I laughed at his pessimistic outlook, thinking how comical he would look with the gas belt wrapped around the outside of a kapok life vest while trying to operate a fishing rod.

The bright morning sunshine beat down as we backed the trailer down the launching ramp at the Seward waterfront. We soon had the boat moored alongside the dock and the pickup stored in the parking lot. After loading our provisions in the boat and making a final check on the weather report, I started the twin Mercury outboard engines and we swung out of the boat basin, headed down the main channel into Resurrection Bay.

I felt a thrill run through me as the wind hit my face; I listened to the hum of the big motors. The boat picked up the steady bounce as we planed over the gentle chop on the bay. I tightened the straps on the kapok life jacket and looked over at Van in the seat to my left. His feet were propped up on the coaming and he lay back in the seat with his hat down over his eyes.

When I saw the new life belt around his waist I decided to dig him about it.

"Say, buddy, hadn't you better put on one of those kapok vests?"

He gave me a startled look. "What the hell for? The belt I'm wearing is plenty good enough."

I laughed. "Whatever suits you, good buddy. I just wanted to make sure you're safe."

He snorted and slid back down in the seat, his hat back

over his eyes. We cruised on down the bay, soaking up the summer sunshine.

After a long run down the bay, I spotted the opening of a cove along the eastern shoreline and swung the boat toward the mouth of the cove. When I throttled back on the motors, Van sat up and looked around. "This looks like a good place to troll for salmon. Let's give it a try."

Climbing out of his seat, he made his way to the back of the boat and rigged two salt water rods for deep fishing. The two lines were soon trailing behind as we idled slowly into the two-mile wide cove. After the choppy water of the bay, the smooth, glassy surface of the cove came as a welcome relief, and I saw Van take off his new life belt and lay it across one of the rear seats near the outboard motors.

"Stop the boat!" Van shouted. I shut down the engines and turned to see what was going on. Van was standing in the back of the boat, a tight grip on one of the fishing rods, and was cranking the reel with vigor. I ran to the rear of the boat and reeled in the other line to give him fighting room. I watched the sharp bow in the rod as he battled to bring in a big silver salmon.

Following a glorious and skillful fight that lasted over twenty minutes, I was able to slip the net under a beautiful sixteen-pound silver that he had managed to bring alongside the boat. Congratulations were due him on his catch, and he got them. We drank a toast of hot coffee for the first catch of the day. His eyes gleamed with fishing fever and a big grin split his sun-tanned face.

After he had had a short rest and wiped sweat off his face, he said, "Well, I think I'll try it again."

He stood up in the rear of the boat, ready to make a cast, and as he flipped the rod over his right shoulder I saw the hook on the end of the line snag the new life belt. The belt sailed through the air, landing in the water some fifty feet behind the boat.

Van stood for a second in shocked silence, then wheeled to face me with a shout: "Turn the boat around! Turn the boat around!"

I jumped behind the wheel and punched the starter buttons and the motors roared into life. Turning the boat around, we drove over to where the life belt had hit the water and stopped. Peering over the sides of the boat we saw the uninflated belt sinking slowly into the deep blue water.

Without hesitation, Van peeled off his shirt and trousers and shoes, then dove over the side, knifing cleanly into the water. I saw the outline of his white undershirt as he dove hard after the belt, but then he turned abruptly and came back to the surface.

He emerged spluttering and flailing his arms, shouting, "Pull me in, quick!"

I grabbed his arms and heaved him over the side into the back of the boat, where he flopped on the bottom of the boat like a big fish.

He rose slowly to his feet. Dripping wet, he was covered with goose bumps all over his skin. His teeth chattered. "I—jiz—it's cold in that w-w-water!"

I couldn't keep from smiling. "Deep, too, ain't it?" Then I helped him out of his wet underclothes, wrapped him in a heavy wool blanket from the forward storage locker, started the engines, and headed for shore.

A roaring fire was soon built on the beach. Van began to thaw out and his shakes gradually subsided. He sat by the fire, deep in thought, and finally spoke: "Why don't we go ahead and cook that silver? I'm hungry."

I agreed and before long had the cleaned fish over the fire on a green stick. As the fish sizzled, I added a little salt, pepper, and sage seasoning, and it wasn't long before we had full stomachs and a renewed outlook on life.

We collected our gear from the beach, extinguished the fire, and climbed back into the boat.

We pushed away from the beach and I put on one of the kapok life preservers and fastened the straps. Without speaking, I reached down into the locker and pulled out another kapok vest and silently held it out to Van.

He looked at the vest and his jaw clamped shut in anger. But after a few seconds his face split in his old familiar grin. He reached out, took the kapok vest, and breathed in.

"Okay, friend, if it makes you happy."

17
Trouble on the High Line

A jangling telephone on my desk in an electric power utility building in Anchorage blew what had started out to be a routine day. My work as representative and photographer for the company resulted in frequent, unexpected assignments, so unforeseen phone calls were nothing new.

Picking up the phone, I looked casually out a window at a bitterly cold morning. With the bright glare of a winter sun on the snow, and exhaust vapors of passing cars and trucks lingering briefly in sub-zero cold, thoughts flashed through my mind of enjoying the quiet swish of snow under my skis as I *schussed* down the high valleys of the Alyeska Ski Resort south of Anchorage.

At the first sound of a man's voice on the phone, I glanced quickly at the pile of paperwork on my desk, but even photographic duties were not, for a split second, enough to erase from my mind pictures of the snow-capped Chugach Range just east of town.

Not until the voice on the phone gave me his message did I know how close I would be to those peaks in the next few hours.

An army helicopter, my informant said, flying patrol in the mountains had just observed two persons on snow machines shooting at the insulator strings on our big high-voltage transmission line that runs through a pass near Indian Creek Canyon. I sat up straight and alert as I learned that several of the insulator strings had been shattered by the high-powered rifle bullets and one of the three cables had been observed arcing. My mind raced briefly over the route of the high line and I thought about all the towns and villages on the Kenai Peninsula which depend on that power line for vital electrical power. A chill ran down my back. What if that line went down and we dropped the load?

Understanding the chaos that might possibly result, I hung up and frantically dialed the number for the line superintendent's office to inform him about the message which had come in. His voice was firm and quick. "Better get your cameras and get ready to roll. I'll get a heavy crew ready to go."

Dropping the phone back onto the cradle, I reached into a filing cabinet drawer and pulled out the traveling bag that contained cameras, film, telephoto lenses, and all the odds and ends used in various conditions involving outdoor photography.

Within a few moments, I was digging through my locker, putting on insulated, down-filled clothing, felt-lined shoe pacs, and a bulky Arctic parka, its hood lined with wolverine fur to prevent frost formation around my face.

Pulling on heavy, fur-lined mittens, I slung the camera bag over my shoulder and headed out into the equipment yard behind the headquarters building. A big line truck sat with its engine idling and on a trailer behind the truck was chained a large Nodwell tracked vehicle, capable of traversing the deep snows and steep grades which we would soon be facing high in the mountains. The men of the crew were busy piling insulator strings and equipment onto the truck and trailer. A few minutes later, the lead man sang out, "Okay, men. Let's roll it."

The truck and trailer, with its five-man crew and me, labored up the steep mountain roads winding back toward the canyon. Studded and chained tires ground and squealed as they fought for traction on treacherous hairpin turns. The truck engine growled as Bill Nash, a big genial giant of a man, shifted into the lower gears to make the grade.

His big hands gripped the wheel with calm sureness as his eyes roamed the peaks and narrow roadway above us. I looked out the right window of the crew cab and saw miles into the distance, where the sun lit the mountains far across Cook Inlet. Then I looked almost straight down at the mountain slope studded with scrub spruce trees. Knowing that Bill's big hands were capable in their task, I felt a sense of security. Sitting beside Bill in the front seat was Abe Newberry, lead man and veteran of many grueling hours and days of high-line work in the mountain peaks and passes. Abe kept up a friendly, easy conversation with the crew and me. I watched the men of the heavy crew, all veterans of years of working under cruel and hazardous conditions. To them, today was just another day of work. They were calm and relaxed, experts in their business. I was unable to detect any apprehension on their faces concerning what might possibly lie ahead.

The grade grew steadily steeper. The truck wheels dug frantically into the deep snow, front and rear axels forcing the wheels to turn. Far above the timberline, the bright sun on the snow was blinding. Without glare-proof safety goggles, we would all have been snow-blind fast.

The truck pulled out onto a narrow, level spot. Abe called out, "Pull her over here, Bill, and we'll unload the Nodwell." Crowding into the side of the mountain trail, Bill shut down the truck and we piled out into snow three feet deep and started loading our lunches and thermos bottles of coffee into the cab of the Nodwell. Bill started the engine on the Nodwell and backed it off the trailer.

Maneuvering with skill and precision, he pulled the Nodwell up near the side of the truck and we all piled into the cab. This time, with a control stick in each hand, Bill gunned the engine and the giant vehicle lurched forward, its wide tracks climbing easily through the deep, soft snow.

We turned off the dirt trail and started up into the canyon, making our own trail. Looking far down the canyon behind us, I saw Anchorage and the upper arm of Cook Inlet in the distance. Looping overhead toward the pass was the mighty 115,000-volt transmission line that had been damaged and might be in serious trouble.

As we climbed steadily toward the pass, I pulled out my binoculars and scanned the double-pole frames that carry the line, looking for the damaged strings of insulators. Far ahead, up near the summit of the pass, I spotted four sets of broken insulators and handed the binoculars to Abe.

He looked up and down the line, then concentrated on the damaged area. Without further conversation, Abe reached for the radio microphone hanging on the panel and pressed the button.

"Anchorage control, this is Fifty-Eight. We'll be working in the vicinity of frames 108 to 112 until further notice."

The voice from the loudspeaker came in clearly: "Roger your location, Fifty-Eight. Anchorage control clear."

The Nodwell came to a stop near the bottom of the first poles holding damaged insulators. We all piled out and gazed up at the shattered bell-string. Listening intently, we heard the unmistakable buzzing of a high voltage arc high at the top of the one-hundred-foot poles. I turned toward Abe.

"It sounds like a rattlesnake I heard once."

Abe's eyebrows moved up with his smile. "Yep. Only this one's bite is a darn sight more fatal."

He turned toward the crew and began to outline the procedures for a change-out of the damaged insulators, while I strapped on snowshoes and started setting up the camera tripod and lenses.

Walking out in a wide circle under the high line, I found fresh tracks of a snow machine. A little farther away, I saw four holes in the snow and dug in the snow with my mittens. In a few moments I held four bright, shiny empty rifle shells in my hand. I slipped them into a plastic bag and then into my pocket for further investigation, then concentrated on taking pictures of the crew in action.

Two linemen strapped on their belts and spurs and started the long, cold climb to the top of the poles. Belting in just under the broken insulators, the linemen then pulled up on a rope the hot sticks and clamps that would hold the massive cable secure while the broken strings of insulators were replaced with new ones. The hot sticks were carefully locked into place, each move planned with cool deliberation and a knowledge that one slip would result in instant death for the men high on the poles.

One of the linemen called down from his lofty perch, "Boy, it's hot up here; I can feel this baby tingle."

"Take it easy, fellows," Abe called back. "We'll have this whipped before you know it."

The moment of truth approached. A lineman, protected with hard hat, rubber gloves, and rubber shirt, reached slowly out with a hot stick and hooked onto the lock pin which held the cable onto the insulators. With a deft pull and twist, he released the pin and the full weight of the cable span sagged onto the hot sticks.

Subconsciously, I had been holding my breath and could feel the tension inside me. The orange-colored hot sticks took the strain and held. I let my breath out slowly. The damaged string was swiftly attached to the rope and lowered to the ground. A new string was hoisted to the top of the pole and locked onto the crossbeam.

Reaching out again with the hot stick, the lineman tried to replace the pin on the cable shackle, but the pin wouldn't go in. Straining against his belt and digging his spurs deep into the pole, the lineman called through clenched teeth, "Jack her up. It won't lock."

The other lineman quickly swung around the pole, swift and sure in his movements, and grabbed the ratchet lever that would raise the hot sticks to where the pin would slip in. With three or four quick twists of the ratchet, the big cable rose inch by inch. The hot stick man watched closely and, at the precisely correct instant, stabbed out with the hot stick, and the lock pin snapped into place.

A deep breath eased out of everyone present. The linemen released the hot sticks and sent them back down on the rope.

Without thinking, I had been taking picture after picture. Now I looked down and saw that the camera had run out of film. As I started to reload with more film, the linemen started down the pole, slow step after slow step. When they reached the ground, sweat was running down their faces, even in the sub-zero cold.

After an hour or more of extreme physical strain and tension, they were exhausted. They climbed into the warm cab of the Nodwell for rest and hot coffee.

After their short rest, the Nodwell moved on up the line to the next set of damaged insulators. The relief linemen started the long climb this time. Three more times in succession, the ritual was repeated and the job was finally finished.

As we rode back down the mountain in the big tracked vehicle, the crew was quiet and conversation was scarce. They were tired; the tension had gone out of them. I rode along, deep in thought, feeling a great sense of admiration for these men. They are men of steel nerves and great physical strength who know danger as a constant companion in their day's work. These are men who, when called on, unhesitatingly climb to the high places, stare death in the face, so that homes, hospitals, stores, and villages in Alaska can continue to receive the vital electrical power necessary to the present-day mode of living.

Bitterness and anger stole over me as I thought of the act of malicious vandalism that had caused five brave men to risk their lives and had required the use of many thousands of dollars worth of equipment to repair the wanton damage. Who would be so foolhardy as to risk a term in the penitentiary or even accidental death by committing such childish acts?

All across America—in the High Sierras, the Rockies, and countless other locations—linemen such as these in Alaska daily perform hazardous duty so that the tranquillity of everyday living may continue for countless numbers of people.

After the Nodwell had been loaded back on the trailer, we turned around and started the truck down the mountain, headed for home. Far below, the rays of a setting sun cast purple and blue shadows across the wide expanse of Cook Inlet and the western rim of the Alaskan Range blazed with the crimson glory of the sunset's afterglow.

In the distance, the lights of Anchorage began to turn on, one by one, twinkling like diamonds. Inside the truck cab, the crewmen were silent, deep in their own thoughts.

Their day's work had been done and rest would be well earned.

18
The Disappearing Frontier

Downtown Anchorage is gripped by the bitter cold of a February morning. A late-rising sun casts its pale light among the buildings lining Fourth Avenue. Exhaust vapors from idling car engines rise straight up among the glittering ice crystals that hang in the air, and the crowds of people along both sides of the street become hushed. . . .

At the far end of the Park Strip, military bands and civic groups form into the opening parade of the Annual Fur Rendezvous. The color guard and the first band in line turn onto Fourth Avenue and the staccato roll of the snare drums sets the cadence for hundreds of marching feet.

The band swings into the rousing strains of a John Philip Sousa march, and the faces of the crowd, hidden by fur-lined parka hoods, light up with smiles of anticipation. The streets are filled with town people, Eskimos, Alaskan Indians, homesteaders, and visitors from great distances.

The fluttering pennants and pageantry of the parade units are matched by the colorful parkas, fur hats, boots, and mukluks of the crowd; many heavy hand-knitted sweaters with their myriad designs are in evidence.

Scattered among the marching bands and parade groups are teams of Siberian and Alaskan Huskies pulling dogsleds. Here and there among the dog teams are the big Malemutes, the half-dog half-wolf combination renowned for strength and endurance.

In restaurants and hotels, waitresses are dressed in the long dresses of the gold rush days, and clerks and bartenders are resplendent in bowler hats, sleeve garters, and string ties. In an air of festivity and holiday merriment, the people of the last frontier have gathered in a traditional celebration as old as Alaska itself.

In a past era, the fur trappers and miners gathered at about this same time each year to celebrate a successful winter catch of furs and to shake off the mid-winter blues, or "cabin fever," as it is called in Alaska. From far canyons and valleys they came, laden with the treasures of their winter labors. For several days and weeks the festivities continued, and the stores and trading posts were piled high with soft, beautiful furs of the lynx, wolf, beaver, ermine, marten, and fox. Miners who had holed up for the winter were part of the colorful scene, and gold dust was much in evidence along with the furs.

During the present day, as in years long past, winter games make up a large part of the festival gathering. Dog sled races are common, and some of the finest teams in the northland compete for rich prizes.

On such a typical February day, the big lead dogs, heads low to the ground and pulling hard, led their teams over the race course, encouraged by the voices of their masters and the rifle crack of the long whip above their heads. Many a driver, having raised his lead dog from a pup, would kneel in front of the lead dog, taking its head in his gentle hands. The silent communication between dog and master would bring a hush over the crowd.

It is usual to see the dogs fret and paw the ground in anticipation as the driver goes back to the sled and the handlers strain to hold the harness of the team. At the crack of the starting gun and the shout of "Hike!" from the driver, the team lunges forward in the harness and the sled races away from the starting line.

The driver, with one foot on the back end of the sled runner, pumps steadily with the other, giving the team all the help possible in the race against time. At the end of the race course, which now averages about twenty-five miles, the teams trot at a steady pace, tongues hanging out, and the drivers alternate between running and riding behind the sleds. Fatigue shows on their faces and their legs ache from the all-out effort.

Near the city hall, part of the crowd gathers to watch the Eskimo blanket toss. A large blanket nearly fifteen feet across, made of many skins, is ringed by over a dozen men, each holding the edge of the blanket in a tight grip. The contestant climbs into the center of the taut blanket and leaps into the air, much the same as a child on a trampoline. With each rhythmic leap, the men ringing the blanket pull harder and harder, until the contestant sometimes reaches a height of twenty to thirty feet with each leap.

The crowd takes up a chant as each contestant tries to out-do the others. Up and down the sidewalks, the crowd is caught up in a holiday mood, punctuated by the laughter and shouts of greetings as old friends renew long-standing acquaintanceships. People throng in and out of the stores, and thousands of mukluks and overshoes squeal on the dry snow underfoot.

In Sidney Lawrence Auditorium, a concert fills the building until there is standing room only. A hush falls over the audience as the conductor walks to the center of the stage, bows to the audience, then raises his baton. A hundred voices rise in close harmony, singing the arias and anthems that have inspired the hearts of men since long before the birth of the United States of America. The people listen in rapt silence to the measured cadence of "Mine eyes have seen the glory of the coming of the Lord. . . ." The thunder of applause rocks the building.

At the Anchorage Historical and Fine Arts Museum, a hushed throng moves slowly through rooms and halls lined with paintings, most of them done by well-known Alaskan artists. Captured on canvas are scenes of the northland, the awe-inspiring colors of famous Alaskan sunsets, the softening shades of mountain glens and the intense blues of lakes and sky. A large painting in the center of a room depicts a setting moon over the rugged spires of Mt. McKinley, while a solitary wolf, surrounded by trackless snow, gazes into the distance.

Gathered in front of the Gilded Cage are a group of Eskimo dancers, decked out with beautiful fur parkas and the traditional mukluks and white ceremonial gloves.

Most of the drummers and dancers are white-haired elders, expert in the songs and chants of their forefathers. The drummers, with their flat, hoop-type drums of animal skin, take up the age-old chants in a sing-song voice, accompanied by the single-note throbbing of the drums.

The dancers sway gracefully, while some of them sit in a semi-circle. Each dance tells a story of some facet of Eskimo life, and the slow, shuffling feet of those standing tell of the hunt for the elusive polar bear, while the seated dancers pantomime the rowing of an oomiak or skin boat which has put into the Bering Sea in search of the walrus and seal.

Still another dance tells of the courtship of youth and the giving of a bride in marriage. Then the tempo of the drums changes and it tells of the death of a chieftain, and the beauty that accompanies the journey of his soul into the faraway spirit land. At the edge of the crowd, a small Eskimo child in her miniature parka watches the dancers with wide dark eyes and chews on the precious candy which stuffs her cheeks.

At night the city is alive with continuous meetings, parties, ceremonies, and dances. In the ballroom of a large hotel a beauty contest is underway. Lithe, curvaceous young beauties vie with each other for awards and recognition. In the dining room of the same hotel, gracious ladies in ball gowns and men in formal dinner wear chat over a five-course dinner. Their conversation is punctuated by the tinkle of wine glasses.

At Anchorage International Airport, the landing lights of huge jet airliners puncture the darkness with brilliant beams of light, while the soft glow of the blue taxiway lights and the runway marker lights stretch into the snowy gloom.

At Elmendorf Air Force Base, two jet-fighter-interceptors create a rolling wave of thunder as their afterburners cut in, launching them into the sky to head for their never-ending patrol along the western edge of the last frontier. In the vast interior of Alaska, a radar operator high on a mountain-top scans his pale-green scope and watches the two tiny blips of the jet interceptors as they move out to relieve their companion sentinels.

Down toward Cook Inlet near the Kenai refineries, a

huge ocean-going tanker nudges easily into an off-shore loading platform. The big hoses are connected and the ship takes on its valuable cargo of petroleum products, pumped from mineral resources buried deep under the tundra and tidelands. Across the wide expanse of Cook Inlet, numerous clusters of lights on the oil well platforms twinkle in the night.

In his endless search for petroleum riches, man has probed deep into the Arctic, drilling beneath the tundra and seas, and has fought the hard rigors of winter storms and ice floes. The search goes on, and long rows of oil pipe continue to grow in the holding yards at Valdez and Fairbanks, and the cargo ships from Japan continue to add to the pile.

While the men, machines, and equipment lie waiting for the signal to begin, the survey crews struggle across the treacherous tundra and bogs, and river valleys and mountain passes, charting the pathway for the largest and most difficult endeavor Alaska has ever known.

Behind survey crews will eventually come the construction crews, their snorting bulldozers plowing a course through wilderness areas which for ages past have known only the passing of the caribou, wolf, moose, and grizzly. After the construction crews have completed their task and gone, Nature will begin its losing struggle to hide the ravages of man.

This slender thread of a pipeline and its companion roadway will open up wilderness areas which are prime summer nesting grounds for the duck and goose, and the moose and grizzly will feel new and increasing pressure from the persistent hunter.

Beyond doubt, America has need of the mineral riches of the northland, but she also has a desperate need to protect inviolate the beauties and treasures of the wilderness.

The mighty bulldozer, symbol of the construction superintendent's dream, is also an emblem of death and destruction to the tundra and forest. The tundra, while maintaining its precarious hold on the centuries-old deposits of glacial moraine, is nonetheless fragile and apparently is unable to recover from the damage caused by heavy construction equipment.

Construction companies now use soft, giant rubber

wheels called rolligons in an effort to minimize damage, and the wide tracks of the Nodwell-type vehicles are favored because of their versatility over various types of terrain. Where once the search for riches was carried out by the lonely trapper and miner, mainly for survival or pursuit of a dream, giant corporations and industries now exert their wealth and political pressure in an effort to force their way into the regions where Mother Nature has hidden her wealth.

Today, all across Alaska, the pacification statements of large industrial and petroleum concerns attempt to lull the frontier residents into believing that industrial progress is necessary for the continued survival of the frontiersman.

A basic rule of survival decrees that a part of every state be set aside for industrial development and improvement of state finances, but the present hue and cry between the state and federal governments has raised some serious questions in the mind of every true Alaskan.

Who is going to have the final word as to how these virgin acres of wilderness will be put to use? The answer to this question will have tremendous impact on the future of many people, and the residents of the State of Alaska will be the ones who will be the most closely involved, both now and in the years to come.

Many of the people I have talked to are worried about whether or not the secretary of the interior will become the final authority in this matter. Most local residents feel the state should have a large voice in how these questions are settled.

The miner and logger are both concerned with earning a livelihood and are looking forward to access to a part of this rich land. I cannot help but recall the sights I saw in very recent years while traveling through the beautiful states of Oregon and Washington. I saw stands of Douglas fir, pine, and spruce which covered countless acres of mountain and valley, and their splendor was unequaled. But I also saw entire mountainsides scourged and barren as a result of "selective logging." These mountains, devoid of all trees and vegetation, had become useless mounds of dirt and granite eroded by wind and sun, and the topsoil was becoming thinner and thinner with every rainstorm and passing season.

No Alaskan frontiersman worth his salt is afraid to face the growing pains of this great and beautiful land, but will the end result of this big struggle be barren mountainsides or possible annihilation of the beauties and treasures of the wilderness?

If we are to call ourselves men, we have no choice but to come up with an answer that is fair and equitable to all concerned, but it must be an answer that will protect one of the finest treasures that we mortals have ever seen or had access to.

The frontiersman, commonly called an Alaskan resident, is an interesting individual. He has come to Alaska mainly to escape the uproar of the big cities and the psychological pressures placed on the individual by trying to keep up with the Joneses as well as the industrial giants who formerly provided his bread and butter.

A true Alaskan is a person who is not concerned with minor discomforts or personal hardships, and who has found a new love in the wilderness and mountains. Unfortunately, mixed among the true Alaskans now are a few misguided malcontents who wander aimlessly about, unwilling to do their share of work.

The old people among the Eskimos, Aleuts, and Alaskan Indians had a form of society that fitted the needs of their situation and environment. They shared a common bond of hardship and survival, and their methods of government were not unlike that of the white man—with his government of the people, by the people, and for the people—in many ways.

Foremost was a respect for parents and elders and a family life filled with love and warmth and tenderness. For those who were ill, aged, or unable to share in the village tasks, there were always food, shelter, and friendship.

During the many years just past, the white man has exposed the Eskimo and Indian to the various ways of "civilization," but has shown little inclination to train the adults in the arts of living in this new way of life.

We have placed them on the "dole" by handing them their needs through various government channels, thereby robbing them of the once-fierce pride that stirred their initiative and intelligence. We have trained their young people in the white man's ways and so instilled in their young the "dog-eat-dog" attitude which has become more prevalent among our own people in recent years.

Now, in the tide of current events, the Eskimo and Alaskan Indian have become enmeshed in a many-sided battle for settlement of their claims of aboriginal ownership of the land. On one hand, the state clamors for land to be set aside for future use and development, while the federal government expresses its concern over lands which it deems necessary for use in carrying out its plans. Meanwhile, self-serving interests have generated friction among the Eskimo and Indian groups, and at the same time are keeping an eye on the potential wealth involved in a pending land claims settlement.

Geological and mineral reports, with their attendant rumors, have whetted a hunger for riches such as Alaska has not seen since the booming days of the Klondike gold rush. This is a hunger that may grow without sanity or reason, and will push into the background all concern for the rich treasures of the lonely canyons, the remote rivers, and wild, lofty, and silent mountains. Industry, with its ponderous advancement of scientific bent, may not see the wide expanse of the nesting grounds of the duck and goose, or the calving grounds of the moose and caribou. In order to propagate the wealth of a mighty nation, are we in the process of giving up a treasure of far greater magnitude, one that will far outlast the profits of oil wells and pipelines?

Far out on the Aleutian chain, a remote and lonely island stands watch over the booming surf and heaving ocean. Until recently, the only sounds were the moan of the winds blowing their gales from the Bering Sea and the stormy North Pacific Ocean and the thundering surf breaking its white waters over the rocks and reefs.

Recently, amid much publicity, huge drilling machines bored deep into the bowels of the earth beneath the island. Lights blazed far into the night as construction crews carried on their unending activity. Big winch drums slowly unwound, lowering deep into the earth a man-made monster with the explosive power of over five million tons of TNT.

Speculation ran wild among the people concerning the possible results of the test blast, and judges in high places contemplated the guarded reports that gave the only indication as to what man could expect from this inferno which took place in a cavern beneath the surface of the earth. While the work continued on the island, the playful sea otters cavorted in the surf, swimming on their backs while they cracked the shells of clams on their chests, dining from the riches of the deep ocean. Farther out at sea, a migrating herd of whales passed slowly by with their rolling porpoise-like gait, and an occasional spout of spray marked the exhalation of the giant mammal. The rocky shores of the island stood as they have stood for centuries of time, still and unmoving.

But for how long will they continue to stand?

Man, in his feeble attempt to master the elements, cannot legislate charity or morality, nor can he improve on the beauties of the handiwork of the Great Creator. But as the eons of history have proven, he will exert his best efforts toward his own destruction, and no words or wishes will sway him. In this most recent day, he has come to disregard selfishly the needs and wishes of his neighbor.

He cannot understand that his rights stop where the other man's rights begin. A current example of this attitude in the Anchorage area, as well as in other places in Alaska, is the manner in which snow machines are used. The snow machine, a boon to a trapper or homesteader, has become a nuisance and a headache of giant proportions wherever and whenever residential areas become covered with the winter blanket of snow.

For some reason, many snowmobile owners have removed the mufflers from the engines and the evening and night hours are hideous with the constant roar of the "iron dogs."

Recent legislation has removed some of the nuisance value of the machines, but every winter brings headaches to the homesteaders and cabin owners in the outlying areas. Police files are filled with reports of bands of young hoodlums riding their snowmachines across posted property, breaking into cabins in acts of thievery and vandalism. There are also documented reports of homesteaders who, trying to defend their property, have been attacked, injured, and hospitalized by hands of snowmachine riders.

Because of the ability of a snowmachine to travel into new and unexplored wilderness areas, these machines have become increasingly popular with hunters and so-called sportsmen. I have witnessed two different occasions within the past winter where hunters on snowmachines have "herded" and chased caribou and moose, running them until the animals dropped from exhaustion, dying with frost-bitten lungs. Needless to say, an animal that has died in this manner is not fit for human use as food, and the carcass lies in the snow to become food for carrion eaters.

Looking back over the history of our own great nation, we see what happened to the herds of bison that once roamed the western prairies. We note also the near extinction of the prairie wolf and the eagle, symbol of the majestic pride of a great empire.

In the great northland of Alaska there remain a few of the rare trumpeter swan, seen occasionally in their annual migration. Among the craggy peaks of the mountain ranges, the bald eagle still wheels and turns on silent pinions, and the lakes and rivers still resound with the seasonal honking of geese and ducks. The lonely, quavering cry of the loon can still be heard on many lakes, and the black bear continues to clown his way through the wilderness.

Along the shoreline of the Pacific Ocean, the giant brown bear still makes an occasional appearance, but his numbers are thinning. The fearless grizzly has yielded to the pressure, and his appearances are becoming limited more and more to the protected areas, such as Mt. McKinley National Park.

Back in the remote areas of the interior of Alaska, the way of the wild remains relatively unchanged, but the new highways and trails are rapidly forcing their way into hitherto undisturbed areas.

Many times in recent months I have heard the comment that these wilderness areas "are of no use to anyone." Surely a thinking person can realize that this last great frontier of Alaska is also the last frontier and fortress of many of the fast-disappearing species that have become legend in the making of our country.